Thirty-two Pa

by Paul Foster Case

Edited by Wade Coleman

April 2023 Edition

Copyright by Wade Coleman

Foreword

Editing Paul Foster Case's Tarot lessons was a well-needed refresher in the fundamentals. It was a joy to edit. Case hid important clues to his *7 Steps* law of attraction techniques until the Thirty-two Paths of Wisdom course – that rascal.

At the end of Chapter 1, Case tells us how to study the 32 Paths.

"To this end, we recommend that the text, which explains the paths and powers to the Hebrew letters, be studied with the corresponding Tarot key. Careful and persistent use of your notebook is an indispensable part of this study."

Therefore, the reader would expect the lessons to contain information about the Tarot Keys, Hebrew letters and their attributions to the Thirty-two Paths. However, that's not always the case.

This book is my notebook, where I fill in the blanks with the Hebrew letters and Tarot keys' attributions.

Also, the 32 Paths of Wisdom lessons can be found on the Internet Archive. Unfortunately, they are missing lessons 14 and 15, so I replaced them with my own text.

To contact the author, write to this email.

DENDARA_ZODIAC@protonmail.com

Acknowledgments

Special thanks to Carol Z for editing.

TABLE OF CONTENTS

THIRTY-TWO PATHS OF WISDOM

CHAPTER 1 – INTRODUCTION

Sepher Yetzirah's earliest manuscript is from 200 C.E. The Thirty-Two Paths of Wisdom probably dates from the 7th-10th centuries. In the Western tradition, the thirty-two paths first appearance was in an appendix of the Sepher Yetzirah by Joannes Stephanus Rittangelius in 1642.

The first paragraph of the *Book of Formation* (*Sepher Yetzirah*) says:

"In thirty-two wonderfully distinguished paths of wisdom did Jah, Jehovah Tzabaoth, the Creative Powers of Life, King of Eternity, God Almighty, Compassionate and Merciful, Supreme and Exalted, Who is Eternal, Sublime, and Holy is His Name, decree and create His universe by means of three kinds of characters: Numbers, Letters, and Words. Ten circumscribed Sephiroth, three Mother, seven Double, and twelve Simple Letters."

In his *Oedipus Aegyptiacus*, Fr. Athanasius Kircher gives a Hebrew text which describes the thirty-two paths and his Latin translation (see Appendix 1). Rittangelius also issued a Hebrew text, followed by Dr. Wynn Westcott, Arthur Edward Waite, Comtesse Calomira Cimara, and Knut Stenring. Ours is based on the Hebrew text's careful study and comparison with other translations into the English tongue.

The student should read the entire text well before taking up the following commentary. The latter is divided into thirty-two sections. Readers with other versions will find this commentary useful in determining whether they prefer our rendering or other translations. We have not quoted these different versions because most readers will profit more by becoming acquainted with one translation.

On the Tree of Life, the ten Sephiroth are shown as circles. The astrological signs or letters are channels that connect the Sephiroth. Both the Sephiroth and the letters are known as "paths."

We retain this ancient designation to avoid confusion in the student's mind when he consults Qabalistic texts. The noun (נתיבים) *nethiboth* means *trodden paths* or *footpath*.

These are paths of *Wisdom* or phases of the manifestation of *Chokmah*, the second sephirah. Thus, in the text quoted above, the Divine Name first mentioned is *Jah* (יה), associated with Chokmah.

The paths of Chokmah are different degrees or categories in the expression of powers attributed to the second sephirah. These are,

1. the power of the fixed stars and zodiacal signs;
2. the power of the life-force.

The power of the stars is the radiant energy that streams from suns. This power is the life-force that animates all vegetable, animal, and human beings. Consequently, in studying the thirty-two paths of wisdom, we are concerned with the thirty-two manifestation of the cosmic life-force.

Every one of the thirty-two paths includes the word *sekhel* (שכל) combined with one or more adjectives. Sekhel means *intellect*, *reason, understanding, wisdom,* and *insight.* It implies practical skill, as does the noun *Chokmah,* Wisdom.

We retain the customary translation, "intelligence," but *sekhel* designates awareness and the ability to use insight practically. To have the power of one of the paths of wisdom implies both knowledge and practical application.

Recall Ehben (אבן) conceals the words *Ab* (אב), Father, and *Ben* (בן), Son. *Sekhel* is a combining *soke* (שך), meaning *booth, enclosure, abode,* with *kole* (כל), meaning *all, the whole, every.* Therefore all the paths are the abode (שך) of the whole (כל) being of the Life-power.

The first letter of sekhel (שכל) is Shin (ש). Its value is 300, and so is Ruach Elohim (רוח אלהים), the Creative Life-Breath. The second letter is Kaph (כ), corresponding to Key 10, representing the universal order's conscious grasp or comprehension. The third letter is Lamed (ל), which Tarot illustrates by Key 11, a symbol of action whereby the awareness symbolized by Kaph is put to work to establish poise and equilibrium in our conscious expression of spiritual powers.

This discourse on the thirty-two paths of wisdom concerns the degrees of conscious awareness manifested by the One Identity in producing the universe and all it contains. These degrees of conscious awareness and activity are the powers of humanity. They are present in every human being. To know what they are, and to live by this knowledge, is to be a practical Qabalist.

Like the Yoga Sutras written by Patanjali, the thirty-two sections of this little treatise are extraordinarily compact. The primary reason is to enable the student to commit them to memory. The secondary purpose is to prevent a superficial reader from understanding the meaning of the text. Nobody can find out what these paragraphs mean unless he takes them as guides for meditation. They are like sign-posts. They show the student in what direction to turn their thought, but words cannot disclose any of these paths' vital secrets. Explanation, commentary, and elaboration are possible, but every student must discover for themselves beyond what may be said or written. This is the real secret doctrine, the mysterious arcanum. Nobody withholds it from you if you do not know it. What bars you from participation in the consciousness of those who know is your lack of determination and skill in managing your mental powers.

We have done what is possible to clarify the ancient text, to make these thirty-two sign-posts legible. To facilitate your studies of the Tree of Life, in parenthesis is additional information.

OBTW.

I added my translation from my studies using Reuben Achley's *The Complete Hebrew English Dictionary*. It is the second translation listed.

1st Path

The first path (Kether, the first sephirah) is called the Admirable or Wonderful Intelligence, the Supreme Crown. It is the light of Primordial Intelligence, and this is the Primary Glory. Among all created beings, none may attain its essential reality.

The 1st Path is the Marvelous Intelligence (Sekhel Mufla). It is the Light of the Primordial Mind. It is the 1st glory. No creature can attain its essence.

2nd Path

The second path (Chokmah) is called the Illuminating Intelligence, and it is the Crown of Creation, and the Splendor of Unity, to which it is the most nearly approximate. In the mouths of the Masters of the Qabalah, it is called the Second Glory.

The Second Path is Illuminating Intelligence (Sekhel Maz'hir). It is the Crown of Creation. It is the Splendor of the Unity(s) and exalted above every head. The Masters of Reception call it the Second Glory.

The third path (Binah) is called the Sanctifying Intelligence, and it is the Foundation of Primordial Wisdom, termed Firmness of Faith, and the Root of thy Mother. It is the *Mother* of Faith, for the power of faith emanates from it.

The 3rd Path is Sanctifying Intelligence (Sekhel haKudash). It is the foundation of Primordial Wisdom and Faithful Faith. It is the basis of faith (Amen) and the **Father** of Faith. By its power, faith emanates (*Atziluth*).

OBTW.

It's **Father** of Faith, not Mother. Rabbi Aryeh Kaplan agrees in *Sefer Yetzirah*, Appendix 2, p. 297.

4th Path

The fourth path (Chesed or Gedulah) is called the Measuring, Arresting, or Receptacular Intelligence, and it is so-called because from thence is the origin of all benevolent power of the subtle emanations of the most abstract essences, which emanate one from another by the power of the Primordial Emanation.

The Fourth Path is the Fixed or Immutable Intelligence (Sekhel Kavua). From it, all spiritual powers emanate as the most subtle emanations. Their powers are from the Original Emanation.

5th Path

The fifth path (Pachad, Geburah, or Deen) is called Radical Intelligence. It is so-called because it is the very substance of unity and is within the substance of that Binah, which emanates from within the depths (literally, "from within the enclosure") of the Primordial Wisdom.

The 5th Path is called Root Intelligence (Sekhel Nishrash). It is the essence of unity(s). Its essence of Binah (Intelligence, Understanding) emanates from the Original Wisdom's refuge (Chokmah).

6th Path

The sixth path (Tiphareth) is called the Intelligence of Separative Influence. It is so-called because it gathers the archetypal influence's emanations and communicates them to all those blessed ones united to its essence.

The 6th Path is the Differentiating Influx Intelligence (Sekhel Shefa Nivdal). It emanates its blessing in abundance, uniting everything in its essence.

7th Path

The seventh path (Netzach) is called the Occult or Hidden Intelligence, and it is so-called because it is the brilliant splendor of all the intellectual powers which are beheld by the eye of understanding and by the thought of faith.

The 7th Path is the Hidden Intelligence (Sekhel Nistar). The splendor illuminates all intellectual powers visible to the mind's eye and contemplation of faith.

8th Path

The eighth path (Hod) is called Perfect Intelligence, and it is so-called because it is the dwelling place of the Primordial. It has no root in which it may abide other than the recesses of Gedulah, whence its essence emanates.

The 8th Path is called the Whole or Perfect Intelligence (Sekhel Shalom). It is the Original Plan. There is no root where it can dwell except in the chamber of Gedulah (Greatness), from which its essence emanates.

9th Path

The ninth path (Yesod) is called Pure Intelligence. It is so-called because it purifies the essence of the Sephiroth, proves and preserves their images, and prevents them from losing their union with themselves.

The 9th Path is Pure Intelligence (Sekhel Tahor). It purifies the Sephiroth (numbers). It tests the law and repairs the pattern. They act in unison without loss of their separate (unique) glow.

10th Path

The tenth path (Malkuth) is called the Resplendent Intelligence and is so-called because it is exalted above every head and sits on the throne of Binah. It illuminates the splendor of all the lights and causes the flowing forth of influence from the Prince of Countenances.

The 10th Path is Scintillating Intelligence (Sekhel Mit.notz.etz). It is exalted and sits on the throne of Binah (Understanding). It illuminates the splendor of all the lights and causes an influx of increase from the Prince of Face.

11th Path

The eleventh path (Aleph, joining Kether to Chokmah) is called the Scintillating or Fiery Intelligence. It is the essence of the veil placed before the dispositions and order of the superior and inferior causes. He who possesses this path is in the enjoyment of great dignity; for he stands face to face with the Cause of Causes.

The 11th Path is the Shining Consciousness (Shekel M'tzuk.tzach). It is truly the essence of the veil which arranges the sequence of the stars. It assigns the Paths their relationships. And (it) stands before the Cause of Causes.

12th Path

The twelfth path (Beth, joining Kether to Binah) is called the Intelligence of Transparency because it is the image of that phase of Gedulah (literally, "of that wheeling of Gedulah"), which is called Chazchazith, the source of vision in those who behold apparitions.

The 12th Path is the Glowing Consciousness (Sekhel Bahir). It is the essence of the Great Wheel (the zodiac). It is called the Visualizer (Chaz.chaz.it). It is the source of vision of the prophets and those who see apparitions.

13th Path

The thirteenth path (Gimel, joining Kether to Tiphareth) is called the Uniting Intelligence, or Conductive Intelligence of Unity, because it is the essence of glory and the perfection of the truths of spiritual unities.

The 13th Path is the Unity Directing Consciousness (Sekhel Man.hig Ha.Achdut). It (*Hu*) is the essence of glory and the reward of the spiritual ones.

14th Path

The fourteenth path (Daleth, joining Chokmah to Binah) is called the Luminous Intelligence because it is the essence of that Khashmal, which is the instructor in the secret foundations of holiness and perfection.

The 14th Path is Illuminating Consciousness (Sekhel Meir). It is the essence of electricity (Chashmal). It teaches the fundamentals of the secret mysteries of the Holy Sanctuary and its plan.

15th Path

The fifteenth path (Heh, joining Chokmah to Tiphareth) is called the Constituting Intelligence because it constitutes creative force (or the essence of creation) in pure darkness. According to masters of contemplation, this is that darkness mentioned in Scripture: "Thick darkness a swaddling-band for it."

The 15th Path is Stable Intelligence (Sekhel Ma'amid). From the pure darkness, it stabilizes the essence of Creation (Briah). The Masters say, "wrapped it in thick darkness." – Job 38:9.

16th Path

The sixteenth path (Vav, joining Chokmah to Chesed) is called the Triumphant and Eternal Intelligence. It is so-called because it is the delight of glory, the glory of Ain, the No-Thing, veiling the name of Him, the Fortunate One, and it is also called the Garden of Eden, prepared for the compassionate.

The 16th Path is Eternal Intelligence (Sekhel Nitz.chi). It is the pleasure (Eden) of the Glory. There is no Glory like it (beneath it). It is called the Garden of Eden, prepared for the Merciful Ones (Saints).

17th Path

The seventeenth path (Zain, joining Binah to Tiphareth) is called the Intelligence of Sensation (or the Disposing Intelligence). It establishes the faith of the compassionate and clothes them with the Holy Life-Breath. It is called the Foundation of Tiphareth in the plane of the Supernals.

The 17th Path is Perceptive Intelligence (Sekhel Ha.Her.gesh). It is prepared for the Faithful Ones so they are clothed with the Holy Spirit. It is called the Foundation (Yesod) of Beauty (Tiphareth) and is placed among the Supernals (upper realms).

18th Path

The eighteenth path (Cheth, joining Binah to Geburah) is called the Intelligence of the House of Influence, and from the interior walls of its perfections, the arcana flow down, with the hidden meanings concealed in their shadow, and therefrom is union with the innermost reality of the Most High.

The 18th Path is called the Intelligence of the House of Influx (Shekel bet ha-shefa). From investigations, a secret is transmitted/attracted to all who dwell/cleave to its shadow. Those who walk the 18th Path bind themselves to investigate the substance (reality) transmitted (emanating) from the Cause of Causes.

19th Path

The nineteenth path (Teth, joining Chesed to Geburah) is called the Intelligence of the Secret of All Spiritual Activities because of the influence spread by it from the supreme blessing and the supernal glory.

The 19th Path is the Intelligence of the Secret of All Spiritual Activities (Sekhel Sod HaPaulot Haruchniot Kulam). The influx permeates from the Supreme Blessing and the Glory of the Most High.

20th Path

The twentieth path (Yod, joining Chesed to Tiphareth) is called the Intelligence of Will because it forms all patterns, and to know this Intelligence is to know all the reality of the Primordial Wisdom.

The 20th Path is the Intelligence of Will (Sekhel HaRatzon). It is the trait from which everything is formed. Through this consciousness, everyone can know the essence of Original Wisdom.

21ˢᵗ Path

The twenty-first path (Kaph, joining Chesed to Netzach) is called the Intelligence of Desirous Quest because it receives the divine influence, which it distributes as a blessing to all modes of being.

The 21ˢᵗ Path is Seeking and Delightful Intelligence (Sekhel HaChafutz HaMevukash). It receives the divine influx to bless all, everyone.

22ⁿᵈ Path

The twenty-second path (Lamed, joining Geburah to Tiphareth) is called the Faithful Intelligence because spiritual powers are increased by it. All dwellers on earth are under its shadow,

The 22ⁿᵈ Path is Faithful Intelligence (Sekhel Ne'eman). It causes spiritual powers to multiply. The Spiritual Ones are drawn close through it, and all find shelter in its shadow.

23ʳᵈ Path

The twenty-third path (Mem, joining Geburah to Hod) is called the Stable Intelligence because it is the power of permanence in all the Sephiroth.

The 23rd Path is Sustaining Intelligence (Sekhel Kayam). It is the power sustaining all the Sephiroth.

24th Path

The twenty-fourth path (Nun, joining Tiphareth to Netzach) is called the Intelligence of Resemblance (or Imaginative Intelligence) because it constitutes the similarity in the likenesses of all created beings.

The 24th Path is Imaginative Intelligence (Sekhel Dimyoni). It gives a form to the imaginations of all Living Creatures.

25th Path

The twenty-fifth path (Samekh, joining Tiphareth to Yesod) is called the Intelligence of Probation or Trial because it is the first test whereby the Creator tries the compassionate.

The 25th Path is Experimental Intelligence (Sekhel Nisyoni). It is the primary test through which all the Merciful Ones become skilled.

26th Path

The twenty-sixth path (Ayin, joining Tiphareth to Hod) is called the Renewing Intelligence because thereby God--blessed be He! -- renews all things begun afresh in the world's creation.

The 26th Path is Regenerating Intelligence (Sekhel MeChudash). By it, the Blessed Holy One regenerates the World of Creation.

27th Path

The twenty-seventh path (Peh, joining Netzach to Hod) is called the Exciting or Active Intelligence because thence is created the spirit of every creature under the supreme orb and the assemblage of them all.

The 27th Path is the Perceptible or Felt Intelligence (Sekhel Murgash). Through it, the senses of all living beings under the zodiac are excited.

28th Path

The twenty-eighth path (Tzaddi, joining Netzach to Yesod) is called the Natural Intelligence because by it is perfected the nature of all things under the orb of the Sun.

The 28th Path is called Natural Intelligence (Sekhel Mutba). It completes and perfects the nature of all that exists under the revolution of the Sun.

29th Path

The twenty-ninth path (Qoph, joining Netzach to Malkuth) is called the Corporeal Intelligence because it marks out the forms of all bodies incorporated under every zodiac revolution and is what constitutes the arrangement and the disposition thereof.

The 29th Path is Physical Intelligence (Sekhel Mugsham). It depicts and establishes the growth of all physical bodies incorporated under the Zodiac.

30th Path

The thirtieth path (Resh, joining Hod to Yesod) is called the Collective Intelligence because astrologers, by the judgment of the stars and the zodiac, derive the perfection of their knowledge of the revolution of ruling principles.

The 30th Path is called Collective or Inclusive Intelligence (Sekhel Kelali). Through it, astrologers study the laws governing the stars and the zodiac and perfect their knowledge.

31st Path

The thirty-first path (Shin, joining Hod to Malkuth) is called the Perpetual Intelligence because it rules the movements of the Sun and Moon according to their constitution. It perfects all the powers of all the zodiac revolutions and the arrangement (or form) of their judgments.

The 31st Path is Perpetual Intelligence (Sekhel Tamidi). It regulates all the cyclic forces that form the revolutions of the zodiac (masloth).

32nd Path

The thirty-second path (Tav, joining Yesod to Malkuth) is called the Serving, or Administrative, Intelligence because it directs all the seven planets' operations and concurs therein.

The 32nd Path is Serving Intelligence (Sekhel Ne'evad). It repairs (Tikun) all the operations of the seven planets and keeps them in their orbits.

THE POWERS OF AN ADEPT

In the Introduction to Transcendental Magic, Eliphas Levi quotes a sixteenth-century manuscript as follows:

These are the powers and privileges of the man who holds Solomon's clavicles in his right hand and the branch of the blossoming almond in his left.

Aleph (א). He beholds God face to face, without dying, and converses familiarly with the seven genii who command the celestial army.

Beth (ב). He is above all afflictions and all fears.

Gimel (ג). He reigns with all heaven and is served by all hell.

Daleth (ד). He disposes of his own health and life and can influence others equally.

Heh (ה). He can neither be surprised by misfortune, overwhelmed by disasters, nor conquered by his enemies.

Vav (ו). He knows the reason for the past, present, and future.

Zain (ז). He possesses the secret of the resurrection of the dead and the Key to immortality.

"Such are the seven chief privileges and those which rank next are as follows:

Cheth (ח). To find the philosophical stone.

Teth (ט). To enjoy universal medicine.

Yod (י). To be acquainted with the laws of perpetual motion and to be in a position to demonstrate the quadrature of the circle.

Kaph (כ). To change into gold, not only all metals, but also the earth itself, and even the refuse of the earth.

Lamed (ל). To subdue the most ferocious animals and be able to pronounce the words which paralyze and charm serpents.

Mem (מ). To possess the *Ars Notaria*, which gives the universal science.

Nun (נ). To speak learnedly on all subjects, without preparation, and without study.

"These, finally, are the seven least powers of the magus:

Samekh (ס). To know at first sight the deep things of the souls of men and the mysteries of the hearts of women.

Ayin (ע). To force nature to make him free at his pleasure.

Peh (פ). To foresee future events that do not depend on superior free will or an undiscernible cause.

Tzaddi (צ). To give at once and to all the most efficacious consolations and the most wholesome counsels.

Qoph (ק). To triumph over adversities.

Resh (ר). To conquer love and hate.

Shin (ש). To have the secret of wealth, always its master and never its slave. To know how to enjoy even poverty and never become abject or miserable.

Tav (ת). Let us add to these three septenaries that the wise man rules the elements, stills tempest cures the diseased by his touch, and raises the dead!

"At the same time, certain things have been sealed by Solomon with his triple seal. It is enough that the initiates know, and as for others, whether they deride, doubt, or believe, whether they threaten or fear, what matters to science or us?"

The powers attributed to an adept are the same as those exercised by the perfected yogi. The magical manuscript quoted by Eliphas Levi is not to be taken literally. In the chapters, we shall make explanations as they seem wise. However, it is for the student's meditation to add to what can or may be written, the inner secrets that cannot be put into words.

To this end, we recommend that the text, which explains the paths and powers to the Hebrew letters, be studied with the corresponding Tarot key. Careful and persistent use of your notebook is an indispensable part of this study.

You will often find no words to express what you know with absolute certainty. In other cases, you may be able to put your knowledge into plain English. Nevertheless, you will perceive the necessity for refraining from writing it.

CHAPTER 2

1st Path of Kether

The Wonderful Intelligence

The 1st Path is the Marvelous Intelligence (Sekhel Mufla). It is the Light of the Primordial Mind. It is the 1st Glory. No creature can attain its essence.

The tables below show the different shades of meaning in the original Hebrew text. The words are arranged for the English reader to read right to left.

ה-נתיב	ה-ראשין	נקרא	שכל	מישכל
the Path	the First	is called	Consciousness / Intelligence	Mind / Intelligence

מופלא	ו'ס'ע	והוא	אור	אין
Marvelous	The highest crown	It is	light	not, no

קדמון	והוא	כבוד	ל-עמוד	על
ancient / primordial	It is	glory	attain	on, to / about

מציאתו	כל	בריה	יכולה	
essence	all	נברא / living creature(s)	can	

27

The 1st Path is called the Admirable Intelligence, the Supreme Crown. As a matter of fact, it is the light that allows us to understand the beginning without beginning, and it is the first glory. No creature can obtain its essence; namely, it is a hidden Intelligence, unclear to anything which is outside it.

Aleph - א

Aleph (א) is the beginning and the origin of everything because it is the model of all letters, and all the paths are contained in it, but universally; from such thing, through metathesis, it is said (פלא), namely, "admirable," which, due to the retrograde meaning is the same as Aleph (אלף), according to that verse: "and His name will be Wonderful, Mighty God, etc."

> For us, a child is born; to us, a son is given, and the government will be on his shoulders. And he will be called Wonderful Counselor, Mighty God, Everlasting Father, Prince of Peace. – Isaiah 9:6.

The first path of wisdom is Kether (כתר), the first sephirah. Kether is the primary condensation of the Limitless Light (סוף אין אור) into a point which is a center of whirling, vortical motion.

Every one of the thirty-two paths of wisdom is fourfold. There is,

Kether in Atziluth, the Archetypal World;
Kether in Briah, the Creative World;
Kether in Yetzirah, the Formative World;
Kether in Assiah, the World of Action or Manifestation.

Every one of the thirty-two paths includes within itself the potencies of all the others. So does every letter. Yet this apparent complexity is simplicity. What seems to be the mazes of a very complicated system are the parts of something relatively easy to grasp.

There is only one Life-power. The four worlds, or planes of activity, are four related modes of this one power's existence. Perhaps a comparison will help you understand.

Below 32 degrees Fahrenheit, water is solid. Water is liquid between the freezing point and that at which it boils. Above the boiling point, it is gas. Yet molecules of ice, water, or steam are chemically the same. Their atoms, however, are composed of protons and electrons. Here we have in ice a correspondence to what Qabalists call Assiah. The fluid state is comparable to Yetzirah, the state of steam to Briah, and the electronic state to Atziluth. This is, of course, only a comparison, but it ought to help you understand the meaning of the doctrine of the four worlds.

Qabalists agree the universe is mental. The world and all its contents are thought into existence by the Universal Mind. Kether in Atziluth is the primary condensation of the Limitless Light into a whirling motion at a point. Kether in Briah is a more definite thought of the same thing. Kether in Yetzirah is an actual center of vortical motion in the plane of super-physical activity, termed *astral* and *etheric*.

Kether in Assiah is a condensation of physical radiant energy at a point that may be as tiny as the focal center of an atom or as large as the central Sun of a world-system, many times greater than our own. For us on earth, our day-star is the Kether of this solar system.

In human personality, the Kether point in Atziluth is the presence of the universal One Self, called Yekhidah (יחידה), the Indivisible. This universal One Self is omnipresent and is therefore centered everywhere.

In humanity, the Kether point in Briah is the Theosophist's "seed atom" continuing throughout our incarnations. It relates to the Eastern schools' term *Ishvara* (supreme soul).

In Yetzirah, the Kether point is the Sahasrara Chakra. This is a center outside the physical body but within the etheric-astral vehicle surrounding the physical body. This "thousand-petalled lotus" is a focus of intense vortical motion. Some writers have made the mistake of supposing this center is within our bodies.

The pineal gland is our point of physical contact with the higher aspects of Kether or Yekhidah. The third eye has not yet evolved to bring the personality into conscious contact with super-physical levels of being. Yet, the pineal gland is the point that corresponds to Kether in Assiah. Like all other aspects of Kether, it is a focal point concentrated in a whirling vortex of radiant energy.

Wonderful Intelligence

Wonderful Intelligence is translated from the word *mopeleh* (מופלא), a variant of *peh.leh* (פלא), used in Isaiah 9:6, where it is the first of a series of names given to one who is also called Shar Shalom (שר שלום), "Prince of Peace."

The text says the Wonderful Intelligence is the light of the Primordial Intelligence. It is a Conscious, Radiant Energy. In whatever world we find it manifest, we are dealing with a living, conscious light. On all planes, the Kether (כתר) point is a contraction of power (כ) at a point of condensation (ת), which, to the successive stages of manifestation, becomes a point of radiation (ר).

Primary Glory

It is also called the Primary Glory. In the original language, this is *kabode rashun* (כבוד רזשן), and the noun כבוד, *kabode* though usually translated as "glory," has for its primary meaning "weight." In passing, note that *kabode* (כבוד) is numerically 32.

Modern physics tells us light has weight or mass. Einstein invented a mathematical formula identifying the universal radiant energy's identity with the mysterious, all-pervading gravitation force. To most of us, Einstein's mathematics is as incomprehensible as would be conic sections to an Australian aborigine.

We say this to show there are living people who can formulate concepts clearly to themselves and their intellectual peers beyond the mental grasp of persons of lesser attainments in that field.

Yet even Einstein cannot solve the mystery of the Primary Glory. Our text says, "None may attain unto its essential reality." It is good to know this because it will save us a lot of time and effort. Created beings cannot attain unto the essential reality of the first path of wisdom because that reality transcends every one of the limitations which characterize "created beings." Whether the method of creation you believe is the instantaneous result of divine fiat or a long evolutionary process, the fact remains that human personalities cannot attain the essential reality of the Primordial Glory. Only the One Reality can comprehend itself.

For human intellect Eliphas Levi says, the existence of this Reality is a necessary hypothesis. Therefore, to experience the beneficent results of conscious contact with the One Reality, Wonderful Intelligence, or another Intelligence associated with the paths, *we must begin by assuming it to be a real presence in our lives.*

Yet this initial assumption is only the beginning. On its practical side, accepting the hypothesis leads to various consequences. Among them is satisfactory knowledge of the real presence of Kether at the innermost center of human personality. This knowledge does not include (and does not need to include) intellectual comprehension of the essential reality of the Life-power. It does include an ever-increasing grasp of the possibilities for bringing the limitless potencies of this presence to effect transformations in human personality. Through the human character, Wonderful Intelligence transforms our society and physical conditions.

Mezla

The radiating energy projected from Kether is named *mezla* (מזלא), translated as *influence*. The root of this term is מזל, which is the singular form of *masloth* (מזלות), literally, wanderers or planets. Thus the force proceeding from the first sephirah is identified with planetary influences. Planets do not shine by their light but by reflecting the Sun's light around which they revolve. That Sun is the Kether of their world-system.

This Mezla is a whirling force, and in its physical expression is the spiraling, electromagnetic energy, which is the substance of atoms that constructs the physical universe. Electrons and protons are whirling energy vortices, moving within the limits of the little "solar systems" of atoms, spinning on their axis.

Kether is the point of projection for three currents of this spiral force. The first pass through the path of the letter Aleph (א), pictured by the Fool. It begins the active manifestation of that aspect of the Life-power known as Chokmah (חכמה), the second Sephirah.

The second channel is the path of Beth (The Magician). It initiates the activity of Binah (בינה), the third Sephirah.

The third projection from Kether carries the whirling force through the path of Gimel to begin the manifestation of the sixth Sephirah, Tiphareth (תפארת), employing the activities symbolized by the High Priestess.

The first Sephirah's three projections of force are not successive in time. They are simultaneous outpourings of energy. The sequence is logical rather than temporal. The same principle applies to projections of force from the other Sephiroth. Thus, for example, the force of Chokmah is projected simultaneously from Chokmah to Binah, Tiphareth, and Chesed through the paths of Daleth, Heh, and Vav; and, in like manner, the force of Binah passes simultaneously to Tiphareth and Geburah, through the paths of Zain and Cheth.

The first three Keys, the Fool, the Magician, and the High Priestess, symbolize the primary differentiations of the influence from Kether. All the other Tarot pictures express the mixture of this primary influence with powers corresponding to other Sephiroth.

The Empress, the Emperor, and the Hierophant carry the influence from Kether. They represent the specialization of influence in the sphere of Chokmah. All three Keys, each in its way, represent the life-power's operation as the masculine, paternal, and procreative influence.

By contrast, Keys 6 and 7, proceeding from the feminine Sephirah Binah, symbolize the operation of the maternal, organizing, formative potencies associated with that sephirah,

These distinctions are worthy of the most careful attention. When you give thought to them, you are by no means devoting yourself to studying a curious, complicated philosophical system. The Conscious Energy flowing from Kether is the animating principle of your human personality. Its various specializations, the ten Sephiroth, and the letters' channels are modes of your life and consciousness. In familiarizing yourself with them and their relations, you obey the ancient maxim, "Know Thyself."

Through the path of Aleph (א), the Kether power is transmitted to Chokmah. Because all powers associated with Chokmah are above the human intellectual level, the Fool is the Tarot symbol of super-consciousness.

Through the path of Beth (ב), the influence is transmitted to Binah, and because Binah corresponds to universal subconsciousness, the path of Beth is a symbol of self-consciousness, mediating between Kether and Binah.

Through the path of Gimel (ג), the influence from Kether passes to Tiphareth. This sixth sephirah is the seat of the Ego of the entire human race – the Son who is "one with the Father (Chokmah)" and equally "one with the Mother (Binah)." Its link with the universal One Self (Yekhidah) is the perfect memory that One Self has of itself throughout eternity. Memory is the fundamental quality of subconsciousness. The High Priestess completes the expression of the power of Kether (superconscious - Aleph. Self-conscious - Beth) by the manifestation of the third potency of universal consciousness, eternally inherent in the Primal Glory of Kether.

2nd Path of Chokmah

Radiant Intelligence

The Second Path is Radiant Intelligence (Sekhel Maz'hir). It is the Crown of Creation. It is the Splendor of the Unity(s) and exalted above every head. The Masters of Reception call it the Second Glory.

הנתיב	ה-ב	'הוא	נקרא
Path	The "2"	It	is called
	second		
שכל	מזהיר	ו-הוא	כתר
Consciousness	Shining	& It is	*Kether*
Intelligence	Radiant		Crown
	Illumination		
ה-בריאה	ו-זהר	ה-אחדות	השוה
Briah	*Zohar*	*ha-Achadot*	It is
Creation	& Splendor	The Unity(s)	
ה-מתנשא	ל-כל	ל-ראש	ו-הוא
exalted	every	head	& It
נקרא	כפי	בעלי	ה-קבלה
is called	by	Masters of	the receive
		(Kabbalists)	Reception
כבוד	שני		
glory	second		

36

Latin Commentary

The 2nd Path is Shining Intelligence. It is the crown of creation and the splendor of the most Universal Unity, which has been raised above any individual. It is called the "second glory" by Cabalists because, being the origin of the entire creation, it is more known than the immediately previous one, that is [אֵין סוֹף] Ain Soph, the hidden Intelligence. So this path is also called "the way of adjustment" by Radak [David Kimhi] in the passage of [Sefer] Yetzirah.

Radiant Intelligence

The second path (Chokmah) is called Radiant Intelligence. Maz'hir (מזהיר) is different from the adjective "Luminous" assigned to the path of Daleth (ד). The light in Chokmah is the original light of Kether, the illumination source for everything below it on the Tree of Life.

Chokmah is the Kether of Briah or Crown of Creation. It is the starting point for the creative series from Chokmah to Malkuth.

From our human point of view, the conscious energy of Chokmah is superconscious. It is the Life-power's knowledge of its nature and powers, transcending every human mental state. In one sense, it is the Life-power's awareness of itself before beginning a cycle of creative activity. Yet we must be careful not to be led astray by our human time concept. Creation is a continual process, going on now just as surely as it did millions of years ago.

The potency of the Life-power is infinite and eternal. No matter how long the cycles of manifestation may be, nothing can exhaust the life-power possibilities. However varied be specializations of the Limitless Light, there have always been, and are now, infinite manifestation options beyond what we know or comprehend. With every moment of time, a new cycle of creation begins. The infinite resources of Life-power cannot be limited by what has gone before. This is the meaning of Judge Troward's statement: "Principle is not limited by precedent."

Consequently, Chokmah, in relation to Kether, is the Life-power's eternal awareness of itself; in this sense, Chokmah is feminine and Kether's mirror. It is the universal consciousness, turned inward and upward toward Yekhidah.

Thus Chokmah is the body of the letter Yod (י) at the beginning of the divine name Yah (יה). The upper point of this Yod is Kether. Chokmah is the initial active point of the Life-power's self-manifestation (Kether) expanded into conscious life powers, which begin all cycles of creation, great and small. The Hermit is a symbol of wisdom. The older man standing on a high peak is the Way-shower and the maker of the path that others climb and for whom he holds his lantern aloft. Meditate on the symbolism of Key 9.

Splendor of Unity

Chokmah is called the Splendor of Unity, *Zohar Achad* (זהר אחדות). Note the Hebrew use of a feminine plural (ות) to indicate the general aspect or quality. Thus the plural form *echadoth* (אחדות), from the singular, echad (אחד), meaning *one* brings to mind that unity is not empty and abstract. It is a unity of unities, a fullness rather than an emptiness.

The divine name assigned to Chokmah is Jah (יה), the shorter form of IHVH (יהוה). Its first letter is Yod (י). Yod is a masculine letter related to the ideas of procreation and the initiation of reproductive processes. Because these aspects of the Life-power's self-expression imply a feminine power of the same quality, the second letter is Heh (ה), which corresponds to Binah, the third Sephirah. Binah is known as Aima (אימא), the mother. Thus the divine name assigned to the second path represents the Life-power as the universal Father-Mother, even though the unique qualities associated with Chokmah accentuate the "Father" idea.

Father is Ab (אב). The first letter, Aleph (א) and Key 0, symbolize super-consciousness. Its second is Beth (ב), and represents self-consciousness, expressed by the Magician. The self-awareness of Chokmah is universal, and the One Self of which it is eternally aware is Yekhidah in Kether.

The number of Ab (אב) and Binah is three (3). Therefore, just as we find it impossible to think of "Father" without having in the background the idea expressed by "Mother," the number of the noun Ab (אב) carries ideas associated with Binah.

The extension of 3 is 6 (1+2+3 = 6). To think of 3 is to also consider the ideas corresponding to 1 and 2. Therefore, the sum of 1, 2, and 3 is 6, the number of Tiphareth, called "Son." Thus, in the title Ab (אב), we have a foreshadowing of the Qabalistic *soul* (Tiphareth), as well as of the *mother* (Binah).

The second Sephirah, Chokmah, is the Sphere of the Zodiac, or fixed stars. In the *Lesser Holy Assembly*[1], from Chokmah comes *mezla* (מזלא), plural *masloth* (מזלות), to refer to the order and arrangement of the constellations or zodiac, Galgal ha-Masloth (גלגל ה-מזלות). [Hebrew doesn't use hyphens. I added here to clarify the Heh (ה) means "the."]

In one sense, masloth represents the New Testament "kingdom of heaven," literally, "kingdom of the skies." In Atziluth, the archetypal world, this is the Universal Mind's idea of the celestial order. This is condensed through the three worlds below the archetypal into the visible constellations in the sky. The motion represented in the heavens' order is the whirling movement, which first manifests in Kether.

When the same whirling force finds expression in organic life, it becomes Chaiah (חיה), the life-force attributed to Chokmah. The Qabalistic conception of life is inseparable from consciousness. The heavens' order is mental, and the energy manifested in that order is radiant, conscious, and vital.

1st Path Projected from Chokmah – Daleth ד

This energy is projected through the path of Daleth into Binah to complete the activity of the third Sephirah. It began with the influence descending from Kether through Beth. Consequently, the Key symbolizing Daleth's path shows a woman crowned with twelve stars, typifying the zodiac. She is pregnant, to indicate that concealed within her is the paternal power of Chokmah (Ab, the

Father). She symbolizes the outcome of the path of Daleth's activity, as manifested in Binah. Note the symbolism of the waterfall (male) and the pool (female) in the Empress. Furthermore, Key 3 corresponds to Ab's number (אב) and Binah (3rd Sephirah). At the Empress's feet is a grain field, representing multiplication (subdivision), one of the ideas attached to the number 3.

2nd Projection – Heh ה

The second path from Chokmah is Heh, symbolized by the Emperor. It carries the influence from Chokmah to Tiphareth. The characteristic of this path is the function of *sight*. Consider this passage from the eleventh chapter of Matthew.

"Everything has been handed over to me by my Father, and no one understands the Son but the Father, nor does anyone understand the Father but the Son and anyone to whom the Son chooses to *reveal* him."

This states the relationship between the Ego of all humanity (Son) and the paternal life in Chokmah (Ab). The verb at the end of the sentence is *reveal* which, in Greek, is connected with vision. The heavens' order is rational and may be perceived through the open eye of reason. Yet this perception requires that we awaken to conscious awareness of the true nature of the human Ego.

Finally, from Chokmah proceeds the path of Vav and the Hierophant. The Hierophant represents Divine Wisdom. The ministers at his feet symbolize knowledge (lilies) and desire (roses) and stand for Chesed's 4th Path. The Triumphant and Eternal Intelligence, expressed by Key 5, is the heavenly order's direct expression. Intuition makes us aware of the correlation of forces. We are struck by its magnificence (Gedulah, one of the fourth Sephirah names) and made conscious of its beneficence (Chesed).

When considering Kether and Chokmah, these are powers resident in yourself. You are a center of expression for the Primal Will, for the ONE SELF. On all planes, your personality is a vehicle for and an expression of the cosmic order. The Wisdom which continually creates the universe has its abode in you. The abiding presence is the Origin of All and the scientific basis for all the works of power and the Magic of Light operations.

Notes

¹ Kabbala Unveiled, Lesser Holy Assembly, Chapter 18

651. But this arrangement is not found in the Most Holy Ancient One. But when that fountain of Wisdom, *Chokmatha* (חכמתא), flows down from *Mezla* (מזלא), the Influence of the Most Holy Ancient One descends from Him. (the previous sentence doesn't read well grammaticallyWhen Aima, the Mother, arises and is included in that subtle ether, then She, Aima, assumes that white brilliance. P. 325

CHAPTER 3

3rd of Binah

The Sanctifying Intelligence

The 3rd Path is Sanctifying Intelligence (Sekhel ha.Kudash). It is the foundation of Primordial Wisdom and the Faithful Artisan (Literally, faithful faith). It is the basis of faith (Amen) and the Father of Faith. By its power, Faith emanates (*Atziluth*).

הנתיב	ה-שלישי	נקרא	שכל
Path	the 3, 3rd	is called	Intelligence
ה-קודש	ו-הוא	יסוד	ה-חכמה
The Holy	& it is	*Yesod*	*Chokmah*
Sanctity		Foundation	Wisdom
ה-קדומה	הנקרא	אמונה	אומן
The Ancient	is called	faith	Artisan
Primordial			
ו-שרשיה	אמן	ו-הוא	אב
& its roots	*Amen*	& It is	father
basis	Faithfulness		
origin	Firm		
ה-אמונה	שמכחו	ה-אמונה	נאצלת
the	מכח	the	*Atziluth*
Faith	by its power	Faith	Emanation

Latin Commentary

The 3rd Path is called the Glorifying Intelligence, and it is the fundament of primary knowledge, which is called the "creator of faith" and its "roots"[amen, אמן], and it is the "mother of faith" because faith stems out from its power. It corresponds to the third Sephira or to the third measure, which is called Binah [בינה], or "Intelligence," because, through it, there is a fulfillment of knowledge for all measures (Sephiroth). First, however, see the book *Baresitich Rabbah* (The Great Genesis)[1], which discusses such discourse profusely.

Sanctifying Intelligence

The third path of wisdom is Binah, Understanding. It is called the Sanctifying Intelligence, Sekhel ha.Kudash (שכל הקודש). The adjective is from a root that means "to make pure, to set apart, to consecrate." The Divine Soul is called The Untouchable Glory of God in Latin. No matter how humanity may "sin," the Divine Soul is the well-spring that cannot be touched by humanity's misinterpretations of reality.

The idea is the selection for specific purposes, combined with perfection. For example, animals intended for sacrifice must be without spots or blemishes. The Sanctifying Intelligence implies something which operates to bring about the best expression of the Life-power's potencies in forms fully adequate for such expression.

In Rosicrucian terminology, the Grade of Master of the Temple is associated with Sanctifying Intelligence, and those who attain this Grade correspond to what the Church calls saints. They are perfected human beings, set apart from the rest of humanity by superior personal development, enabling them to exercise unusual mental and spiritual powers.

Binah is the field of separative activity, whereby the infinite possibilities of the Life-power manifest in a multiplicity of finite, specialized forms. Thus the idea of multiplication associated with the number 3 is connected with subdivision. The One Reality does not lose its unity through the creative process of subdivision or specialization. For example, the idea of sitting can be expressed through an endless variety of chairs, stools, benches, etc., so that which is behind any specific forms is One. However, many variations may result from it.

These possibilities in the Universal Mind are within Chokmah. They are actualized in Binah. In Chokmah, the Universal Mind looks into itself. In Binah, the Universal Mind looks into the field of manifestation and perceives the logical consequences of the possibilities it discerned in Chokmah.

The power of specialization is personal as well as universal. The Pattern on the Trestleboard says we are filled with Understanding and under its guidance, moment by moment. We are unaware of this guidance until we reach a certain measure of ripeness. We believe ourselves to be autonomous, self-directed beings gifted with personal free-will.

As we grow riper, we understand our error. We know it intellectually long before we have higher consciousness experiences of the vivid realization of mystical union with the ONESELF.

Test and trial convince us that we may link ourselves to a super-personal source of power (Key 1, Beth, joining Kether to Binah). Furthermore, training in creative imagination allows us to adapt our mental states and harmony with the cosmic order. It is symbolized by Key 3, the path connecting Chokmah to Binah. As we gain skill in using our mental powers, we find that our environment's external conditions shape themselves (as it seems) by our mental patterns.

Whatever understanding of these truths you possess begins as an intuitive perception; you didn't manufacture it. It came to you from something deeper and higher than your intellect. It is the Sanctifying Intelligence manifesting through Neshamah, the Divine Soul. The single Divine Soul never ceases to be ONE. The Divine Soul omnipresence dwells simultaneously in all souls, incarnate and discarnate, human and non-human. This scheme has non-human personalities, some below and others above the human level. Others are part of streams of evolution parallel to humanity.

As we experience the truth that we are in touch with something higher and have a practical demonstration that our mental patterns take form, we grow in confidence.

Firmness of Faith

The third path is the Firmness of Faith and the Father of Faith. Faith is more than assurance. It is a power that can produce psychological and physiological manifestations. Faith cures ailing bodies and minds and heals diseased circumstances. Faith enables those who have attained full ripeness to perform works of power beyond the accomplishments of average men and women. These works of power are accomplished as a fulfillment of the law, and faith is the power that makes these works possible.

Two paths lead from the Sanctifying Intelligence and communicate its influence to Sephiroth below it. One carries the Sanctifying Intelligence's power down to Tiphareth and links the Divine Soul and the Ego. The other carries the power from Binah down to Geburah and links the Divine Soul and Volition.

1st Path Projected from Binah – Zain ז

The first of these is the path of Zain, symbolized by Key 6, The Lovers. The angel Raphael (God as the Healer) stands for the descent of Kether through Beth, whereby the One SELF is manifest in Binah as Neshamah, the Divine Soul. The woman in Key 6 is the Great Mother, Binah, as the agency whereby the One Self's power is communicated to the Ego in Tiphareth. The man is Adam, the Ego in Tiphareth.

2nd Projection – Vav ו

In Key 7, the houses in the background refer to Beth, which joins Kether to Binah. The walled city refers to Binah, Mother. Great Sea and Holy City are names for Binah and the Sanctifying Intelligence. With other design details, the chariot and the charioteer give a martial aspect to this Key 7. The background relates to the Sephirah from which the path of Cheth begins. The foreground refers to Mars, the seat of volition, where the path of Cheth is completed.

The divine name Elohim (אלֹהים) is assigned to the third path. It is plural, following the idea that the three Sephiroth on the same side of the Tree as Binah are associated with multiplicity. Elohim is the divine name associated with creation in the first chapter of Genesis. Elohim is divine self-expression, just as Jah (הי) and Jehovah (יהוה) are names connected with divine self-realization.

Notes

[1] *Baresitich Rabbah* is a Talmudic midrash interpretation of the Book of Genesis.

The 4th Path – Chesed

The Fixed or Permanent Intelligence

The Fourth Path is named the Fixed, Permanent or Intelligence (Sekhel Kavua). From it, all spiritual powers emanate as the most subtle emanations. Their powers are from the Original Emanation.

שכל	נקרא	ה-רביעי	ה-נתיב
Intelligence	is called	the 4, 4th	the path

שממנו	כן	ונקרא	קבוע
from which	yes, so	& called	Constant
			Permanent

ה-רחניות	חכתות	כל	מת-אצלים
spiritualization	powers	all	Emanation
	forces		

אלו	שמת-אצילות	ה-אצילות	ב-דקות
These	Atziluth - Emanation		subtlety
			fineness

ה-קדמון	ה-מאציל	ב-כח	מאלה
Ancient	אציל	force	From these
Primordial	Emanation	power	

49

Latin Commentary

The 4th Path is called the Intelligence of "Destination" or "Guidance" because all the spiritual virtues, by their subtility, stem from it, as they are brought towards it, as being a goal, by the higher Intelligences; from it, one thing comes out from the other, by virtue of the Supreme Crown, and it is called "ideal flux."

Permanent Intelligence

The fourth path originates all spiritual (ethereal) powers that emanate as the most subtle emanations. These are powers of Chokmah, forces of the universal light-force, which is the life-force of humanity. They are benevolent powers symbolized in Key 5 and the path of Vav (ו). This path carries the influence of Illuminating Intelligence from Chokmah to Chesed. This is expressed by the receptive ministers kneeling at the feet of the Hierophant. The Hierophant symbolizes the powers of Chokmah, Wisdom.

These powers emanate from one another by the Primordial Emanation, Kether. Its energies are carried from the first Sephirah to Chokmah through Aleph (א), corresponding to the Tarot Fool.

These spiritual powers are modes for the expression of your life-force. They are subtle essences because they are subdivisions or specializations of the life-force, like waves in an ocean, or currents within it, though not separate from the sea's whole expanse and depth.

Chesed – Seat of Personal and Cosmic Memory

The fourth Sephirah (Chesed) is the seat of memory. This includes cosmic and personal memory. The Life-power's perfect recollection of itself and its potentialities, and the entire sequence of events in the creative process, is the basis for the continuity of the cosmic order.

Laws of nature are rooted in this cosmic recollection, and the dependability of these laws has its basis in this cosmic memory. Our human memories can be extended by yoga and related forms of mental practice, which enable us to get below the personal level of recollection into the cosmic memory. Other techniques are used without conscious awareness of what is being done. Scientific discovery participates in the Life-power's perfect memory of the creative order.

From the fourth Sephirah, the path of Teth (ט), illustrated by Key 8, Strength, carries the Fixed or Permanent Intelligence's influence into the fifth Sephirah. It mingles with the forces descending to Geburah from Binah through the path of Cheth. When we study the fifth Sephirah, we'll consider this more detail.

In the symbolism of Key 8, the woman who tames the lion corresponds to the feminine aspect of Chesed. Every Sephirah is receptive, or feminine, to the one that precedes it. And every Sephirah is projective, or masculine, to those that follow. The red and fiery lion corresponds to the Mars force active in Geburah. The woman symbolizes subconsciousness and memory, assigned to the fourth Sephirah.

Benevolence

The text says, "From it, all spiritual powers emanate as the most subtle emanations." From Chesed emanates an exceedingly fine substance having mass and weight. Benevolent thought and speech have actual weight and set up movement of actual substance. The blessings the Chasidim shower on those who enter into relation with them are no abstractions. They are projections of real substance.

Act as if you were perfectly sure of it to keep in contact with Eternal Supply. Give your time, knowledge, interest, and possessions freely. Freely, yet not wastefully. Give as intelligently as possible, where the gift fills a real need. Then, let go of whatever you have given, leaving the recipient of your benevolence to use the gift as he sees fit. Learn this fine art to become one of the Chasidim, having free access to Eternal Supply's limitless treasure.

2nd Projection – Yod ＇

The second path proceeding from Chesed is Yod, illustrated by Key 9, The Hermit. Through it flows the influence from Chesed (cosmic memory) to Tiphareth (Ego). In Key 9, the Hermit looks down a path that his footsteps have made. It is a symbol of memory. In Key 9, the masculine aspect of Chesed has emphasis because Yod attributed to this Key. Yet, there are traces of feminine concepts in Key 9 in its relation to Virgo.

3rd Projection – Kaph כ

The third path proceeding from Chesed is Kaph, illustrated by the Wheel of Fortune, Key 10. The number 10 is the extension of 4 $(1+2+3+4 = 10)$. Furthermore, Chesed is the Sphere of Jupiter, Key 10, and Kaph is attributed to Jupiter. This third path from Chesed ends in Netzach, the seventh Sephirah, the seat of humanity's desire nature.

Next, we study the fifth and sixth paths and the Tarot Keys leading to and from them. Beginning with Tiphareth, we are concerned with powers and principles belonging to the field of human personality, as most of us know the human character. After studying the ten Sephiroth and their paths, we will study the letters and their paths. In that part of our work, we find many hints concerning occult forces' practical use and direction.

CHAPTER 4

5th Path of Geburah

The 5th Path is called Root Intelligence (Sekhel Nish.rash). It is the essence of unity(s). Its essence of Binah (Intelligence, Understanding) emanates from the refuge of the Original Wisdom (Chokmah).

שכל	נקרא	ה-חמישי	ה-נתיב
Intelligence	is called	the 5, 5th	The Path
מפני	כן	ו-נקרא	נשרש
because	so	& called	root, basis
			foundation
השוה	ה-אחדות	עצם	שהוא
That	unity(s)	essence	It is
ה-בינה	ב-עצם	מיועד	ו-הוא
Binah	essence	designated	& it is
Understanding			
ה-קדומה	החכמה	מגדר	ה-נאצלת
Ancient	Chokmah	enclosure	Atziluth
Primordial	Wisdom		Emanation

Latin Commentary

The 5th Path is called Radical Intelligence because it is the very Universal Unity, which aggregates itself with that [בינה, Binah] Intelligence, which stems from the most internal parts of the primary knowledge. The virtues, taken from the higher paths to this fifth path and herein clinging, have become equal when carried from this path to the inferior ones. They pass, and they are transformed, according to the different behavior of men, into clemency or severe judgment; see Pardes[1] about such matters.

Root Intelligence

The fifth path of wisdom (Geburah) is called the Root Intelligence, *Sekhel Nish.rash* (שכל נשרש). The first three letters spell *nasher* (נשר), eagle, a symbol for Scorpio. It governs the reproductive power used in practices that lead to conscious union with the Cosmic Will.

Mars rules Scorpio. Geburah, the fifth sephirah, is the Sphere of Mars. To Geburah is attributed volition, the Life-power activity, which gives humans the feeling that we have a "personal" will.

When *nasher* (נשר) is separated from the rest, what remains is Shin (ש), attributed to Fire, which is also associated with Geburah. Shin is numerically 300, and so is Ruach Elohim (רוח אלהים), Spirit of God or Holy Spirit. Therefore, *nasher* Shin (נשר ש) is "Eagle of the Holy Spirit." Qabalists hide occult meanings behind the outer veils of language.

"Eagle of the Holy Spirit" refers to the idea that the Life-power is reproductive, creative, and formative. It continues and multiplies its characteristics through self-expression. The Bible emphasizes God's transcendence but includes passages that humanity is the offspring of a deity and not merely the work of God's hands. Humans are inherently divine. Only the thinnest veils are drawn over this doctrine.

The eagle stands for Scorpio, which links the phrase, Eagle of the Holy Spirit, to Key 13, Death. Also, the Shin (שׁ) is illustrated in Key 20. Study these two Keys together. The conscious immortality symbolized by Key 20 is a consequence of the direction of the force, which is the active principle expressed by Key 13.

This force is connected with the feeling of personal will and muscle tone. Flabby muscles and weak will characterize the sexually incontinent. The name Geburah is from the adjective *geh.ver* (גבר), signifying a *strong man* or *stud* (Alcalay).

The text says the Root Intelligence is the "essence of unity." Unity here means Kether and suggests the force of the fifth path is Mezla (מזלא) because the primary whirling motion begins in Kether. Again, the text says that Conscious Energy is the substance of all things.

On the Tree of Life, the substance aspect of this energy is represented by Binah (3rd sphere), of which Geburah (5th Sephirah) is the direct reflection. Root Intelligence is within the substance of Binah, and Binah emanates from within the Primordial Wisdom. Therefore, the text links Kether's (unities) ideas, Chokmah, Binah, and Geburah. This strongly suggests that the ten Sephiroth are not separate entities but ten ways the human mind conceives a single reality.

Also, Chaiah is the Life-force seated Chokmah. In Geburah, the Life-force is specialized as Mars, which is the basis of our feeling of willpower. The emotion dominant in calling forth volition is the flight/fight response. Fearing starvation, we hunt for food. Fearing enemies, we engage in warfare. Fearing our name will be forgotten, we have children to perpetuate and continue our name.

In hunting and fighting, we develop courage and strengthen our will. Whether we fight or run depends on glandular secretions from the gonads and adrenals, both ruled by Mars. One name for Geburah is Pachad (פחד), *fear*. Real courage is not to be confounded with fearlessness. The world's bravest soldiers and adventurers have confessed they are far from fearless. They face what they fear and fight it. The coward runs.

Violation

The cosmic life-force, seated in Chokmah, is the immediate source of the feeling of "personal will." Our sense of willpower is due to tensions in our bodies as the cosmic life-force plays through them. All personal activity is due to various resistance that the human organism offers to the life-force's flow. Our bodies (physical bodies and finer bodies) perform their various functions because they are arranged to provide specific types of resistance to the flow of the current of the Life-power.

When, despite fear, we face our adversaries and meet them courageously, we find means to overcome them – to bring them over to our side. Thus, the fifth Sephirah's name corresponding to man's highest thought concerning this path is Deen (דין), meaning *justice* and *law*.

What motivated the United Nations in World War II? Primarily fear of being enslaved by the Axis Powers. Fear led to the will to win. It was backed by the production of war materials and the training of our strongest men for battle. Though the military victory was ours, it is evident that unless it leads to establishing a just and lasting peace throughout the world, it will be a hollow triumph and a prelude to an even more devastating holocaust.

We must bring our present enemies over to our side by demonstrating the superiority of the way of life we fought for. Not by loudly asserting that ours is the better way. Not by trying to force "the American Way" on the rest of the world. Force may be necessary, for decades, to police the world, but not until a world republic is established can there be lasting peace.

This will not be done in a day. Several generations must give their best efforts to bring lasting peace. It will take courage, sacrifice, and goodwill. It will require the maximum exercise of intelligence, patience, and skill. Yet, it can be done if there is an honest will to do it. William James said men need a substitute for war. Establishing social justice for all people, regardless of race, creed, or color, calls for even greater courage and skill than required for combat. Every field of science and art has something to contribute to this enterprise. All types of expertise may be utilized in this undertaking. Here is a new frontier, beckoning to all adventurous spirits.

Among them, occultists have many opportunities. Those fortunate enough to understand how to evoke and direct the subtle powers latent in humanity have much to offer. The movement for establishing a New Order of the Ages began with the American Revolution. Its inception in the Western School of occultism was based on qabalah and hermetic science. As the inheritors of this wisdom, we have much to do with extending the gift of freedom to all humanity.

Behind the veil of appearances are hidden the workings of absolute justice. The laws that govern the universe will destroy the folly of the delusion of separateness. Therefore, the fifth path is called Root Intelligence, for those who know and act with the knowledge that willpower possesses the very root of freedom. It is the delusion of separateness that breeds wars and enslaves humanity. The certainty of non-separateness liberates. When its social, economic, and political consequences are seen and made realities, the result will be lasting peace.

No one lives to themself, thinks, or acts to themself. They who have a vision of the truth of non-separateness exert tremendous influence on the thinking of their contemporaries. When someone has the knowledge and skill to increase their mental broadcasting range and intensity, they are called to one of the most valuable and interesting works of practical occultism.

This work belongs to the Grade of Greater Adept. Practice in this Grade involves exercises that enable the adepts to identify their *personal* volition with the *One Will* manifest in the cosmic order. Much of this practice depends on evidence supplied by science, which demonstrates that our activities express unaltered laws of the universe. Familiarity with this evidence helps the Greater Adepts dispel the delusion that their thoughts, words, or deeds originate inside their skull or skin. Through observation, the Greater Adepts see their personality as the vehicle or instrument of the Divine Soul. This is symbolized by Key 7 and the eighteenth path of Cheth (ח), carrying the influence from Binah to Geburah.

Therefore, this practice's first consequence is the Greater Adept becomes a conscious administrator of cosmic justice. They train themselves to regard all their actions and work as a personal expression of universal laws. When they act, they bring all their powers of mind and body. Through meditation and reflection, they make habitual the thought that whatever we think, say, or do is accomplished through their personality rather than by it. The Greater Adept's life is devoted to manifesting Divine Justice. Key 11 represents this mental attitude and is symbolized by the feminine figure. The woman in Key 11 has yellow hair, like the Empress and the chariot's driver in Key 7. Yellow is Mercury in the tarot color scale. They all have headdresses that bind the hair. This symbolism is intended to show that Key 11 represents a *habitual mental* attitude maintained automatically because it is *subconscious.*

Through the 22nd Path corresponding to Key 11, the power of Geburah is carried to Tiphareth. This completes the six descending paths into Tiphareth originating in the paths above. The first path to the Sixth Sephirah is that of Gimel (ג) and the High Priestess, initiating the activity of Tiphareth as the seat of the One Ego for all humanity. The Ego is the Qabalistic and Christian "Son," who is "one with the Father."

The second path which leads to Tiphareth is Heh (ה) and Key 4, which links the cosmic order and power of Chokmah to the One Ego. The third path from above is Zain (ז), illustrated by the Lovers. From Zain, the influence of the Divine Soul in Binah is linked to the One Ego. The fourth path carrying power to Tiphareth from above is Yod (י) and Key 9. It conveys to the One Ego the influence of Chesed, and endows the Ego with the riches of the Universal Mind's perfect recollection of itself and all its powers.

The 23rd Path proceeding from Geburah is symbolized by Key 12. Through it, the influence from Geburah passes to Hod. The Hanged Man is a further development of what is shown by Key 11. The Greater Adept suspends all ordinary notions of personal activity. They are confident they do nothing by themselves. They rest securely in their knowledge that universal life and law support them. They are *adepts bound by their engagements* because all personal activity is seen to be *engaged* to the other activities of the cosmos, just as a wheel in a watch is *engaged* to the rest of the works and moved by the power of the mainspring. Note the Hanged Man is pictured as a pendulum. This symbolism was intended to suggest the *clockwork* simile we employed here.

[1] **"Pardes"** refers to (types of) approaches to biblical exegesis in rabbinic Judaism or interpretation of text in Torah study. The term, sometimes also spelled **PaRDeS**, is an acronym formed from the same initials of the following four approaches:

- **P**eshat (פְּשָׁט) – "surface" ("straight") or the literal (direct) meaning.
- **R**emez (רֶמֶז) – "hints" or the deep (allegoric: hidden or symbolic) meaning beyond just the literal sense.
- **D**erash (דְּרַשׁ) – from Hebrew *darash*: "inquire" ("seek") – the comparative (midrashic) meaning, as given through similar occurrences.
- **S**od (סוֹד) – "secret" ("mystery") or the esoteric/mystical meaning, as given through inspiration or revelation.

- Wikipedia

6th Path of Tiphareth

The Differentiating Influx Intelligence

The 6th Path is the Differentiating or Mediating Influx Intelligence (Sekhel Shefa Nivdal). It emanates its blessing in abundance, uniting everything in its essence.

שכל	נקרא	ה-ששי	ה-נתיב
Intelligence	is called	sixth	The Path
ו-הוא	ה-אצילות	נבדל	שפע
& It is	*Atziluth*	discern, separate	influx
	Emanation	distinguish, distinct	
כל	על	ה-שפע	משפיע
all	on	influx	influencing
everything			giving in abundance
	ב-עצמו	ה-מתאחדות	ה-בריכות
	in its essence	unite, uniting	Blessings

Latin Commentary

The 6th Path is called the Intelligence of the Mediating Influence because the emanations' flux is multiplied in it. It makes it so that this inflow shall flow in all containers of blessings united in it. This one is called the "path of water."

The 6th Path of Tiphareth

The sixth path synthesizes the first five Sephiroth powers, from Kether to Geburah. In Tiphareth are concentrated the power of the Primal Will of the One Self (*Yekhidah,* unique essence) carried through the path of Gimel (ג). Through the path of Heh (ה), the life-force (*Chaiah,* living essence) flows into Tiphareth. The Mezla that keeps the stars in their place is the same mainspring in every human life. The Divine Soul's influence, *Neshamah,* is the overshadowing presence pictured as an angel in Key 6.

Through Chesed, Yod's (י) path carries the awareness of past events and their relation to one another, symbolized as the Hermit.

Human volition is pictured by Key 11. The subconscious operation of the law of justice directed by the Divine Soul (Neshamah) is portrayed as the Empress in Key 3. Key 6 is shown as the angel, and Key 7 is the rider in the chariot.

Tiphareth is central to the Tree of Life. It is like a reservoir into which are poured the influences of the five Sephiroth above it, and from which flow, by way of the paths of Nun (נ), Samekh (ס), and Ayin (ע), the powers active in humanity's desire nature, intellect, and the Vital Soul that we share with terrestrial organic life. Hence the sixth path of wisdom is called the Intelligence of the Differentiating or Mediating Influx Intelligence.

Differentiating or Mediating

The name for this path is derived from the central position of Tiphareth. It collects the descending powers from above and distributes those powers through the channels, which are below.

Nivdal (נבדל) means *distinct, separate, discern, distinguish*. Differentiating Intelligence is a discriminative consciousness. The power manifest in our personality classifies the various objects of experience.

In the plane of creative thinking, this discriminative quality of the Ego is the power that classifies various objects of thought and imagination. In Briah, the image-generating faculty of Tiphareth within us gives shape and diversity to the archetypal principles flowing into our field of awareness.

This is one reason the sixth Sephirah is named Adam (אדם). Genesis says the Lord brought all creatures before Adam to be named, and whatever Adam called them, that became their name. So the Namer, in human personality, is the central Ego.

Time

The Garden of Eden, or "garden of delight," is related to time because Eden (עֵדֶן), read with other vowel points, means *time*. Adam was placed in the garden to dress and keep it. The secret doctrine here concerns the One Ego of humanity and its time concept.

The human time sense is bound up with our recurring experiences of night and day, lunar phases, and the order of the seasons. It is a time sense peculiar to us as earth-dwellers. One might almost say that our "time" is something invented. And we have become slaves to our invention. Nevertheless, the investigators seeking to explain the psychology of mystic experience soon realize that the idea of time is transcended by those who enter a higher order of knowing.

The recollection of past lives is overcoming the limitations of our time concept. When it occurs, the past becomes the present in the consciousness. Prediction of the future is the reverse of this.

A seer perceives as existing now what other people consider the future. The whole past or future exists now as an all-inclusive reality, present as a whole to the Universal Mind. This may be too simple a way to express it. We deal with something which eludes even the most careful and subtle words. If we consider what Poe calls "thought of a thought," we will not fall into the error of supposing what has been said to be a complete explanation.

The One Ego seated in human hearts has a different time concept from most humans. Jesus' remark illustrates this, "Before Abraham was, I am." He who experiences the knowing characteristic of the Lesser Adept has some knowledge of Jesus' statement. It may be only a glimpse or a series of visions that give the adept a different time concept.

Jesus instructed, "Whatsoever things you ask and pray for, believe that you receive them, and you shall have them." He did not attempt to explain this instruction. Instead, he told his hearers what to do to establish dominion over circumstances, which is the Lesser Adept's main work. Those who follow this instruction act on an assumption they do not understand. Still, because it is a correct assumption, they speedily accumulate a store of experience, which teaches them the value of adopting this mental attitude.

One result is that they rid themselves of impatience. They are free from hurry. They become true believers: "He that believes shall not make haste (be stricken with panic)." – Isaiah 28:16.

When we feel pressed for time, skill and precision in action are diminished. Thus Eliphas Levi says a magician should work as if he had all eternity to complete his undertaking. Likewise, the New Testament teaches eternal life, which participates in a living consciousness different from our ordinary time-bound interpretations. The Fool's girdle symbolizes time. When the girdle is removed, his outer garment of black and red, denoting the union of ignorance and desire, may be removed to leave him clad in the white robe of wisdom.

The sixth path gathers together the emanations of the archetypal influence. The archetypal world powers are outside the limits of time. The One Ego is outside time limits. Melek (מלך), the king, a title of Tiphareth, is also above and beyond our time concept. Adam is king, exercising dominion over everything below the egoic level because the EGO-consciousness is free from the delusions rooted in the idea that the past was and the future is to be, while only the present is actual and real.

1st Path Proceeding from Tiphareth – Nun נ

When the eternal consciousness of the One Ego finds expression through a human personality, its first consequence is a change in that person's ideas about death. This is what is symbolized by Key 13 and Nun. The Sun, rising behind the landscape in Key 13, refers to the dawn of a new time concept. In the early morning, the rising Sun shows that the full awareness (pictured in Key 19) is not yet manifest. The Sun refers to Tiphareth, which is the source of the path of Nun.

The skeleton repeats some of the conventional symbolism associated with time. It wields a scythe (Saturn) and is symbolized as the reaper – Father Time.

2ⁿᵈ Path from Tiphareth – Samekh ס

The second path proceeding from Tiphareth is Samekh, illustrated by Key 14. The crown in the background is Kether. Tiphareth is placed, with the path of Gimel (ג) above and the paths of Samekh (ס) and Tav (ת) below on the middle path of the Tree of Life with Kether at the top. The path in Key 14 stands for the two paths above Yesod, and the pool at its lower end is Yesod, the seat of the Vital Soul. On one side is an eagle indicating Scorpio and Nun's path. On the other is a roaring lion, a conventional symbol for the devil, so this lion corresponds to the path of Ayin (ע) and Key 15.

The angel is Michael, and the solar disk on his brow identifies him as representing the powers of Tiphareth (Sphere of the Sun). The Holy Guardian Angel is the One Ego, the true Actor and Knower, manifesting its consciousness and energy through humans' awareness and activity. The Vital Soul's operations and automatic consciousness are modified by devoting our actions to this Holy Guardian Angel's direction. The practice of devoting all personal actions, both mental and physical, to the One Self brings about the automatic consciousness's purification. The inevitable result is an alteration of the habitual, subconscious time concept.

The last path proceeding from Tiphareth is Ayin, illustrated by Key 15. This path and its Key have to do with the means whereby the Ego in Tiphareth changes our intellect, which corresponds to the eighth Sephirah (Hod), at the lower end of the path of Ayin.

The skeleton in Key 13, the angel in Key 14, and the devil in Key 15 are not three different things. They are three aspects of the One Ego, as that Ego appears to be personal consciousness. In dealing with Key 15, understand that the devil is the Master of the Game. He represents the way the One Ego appears to the ignorant. He symbolizes the threatening lion of Key 14. Yet, the Master of the Game brings about humanity's intellectual development.

For this reason, the symbol of Mercury is prominent on Key 15. We develop intellectual power by meeting and solving problems that threaten us. As long as we accept our environment's superficial appearances at face value, our intellect does not evolve. So long as we believe in evil spirits or a single Lord of Evil, attended by hosts of malicious imps, we cannot glimpse the Eternal Splendor corresponding to the eighth Sephirah.

Humanity's Evolution

The royal power seated in our hearts will not let us rest. It prods us into investigation and action. It frightens us into doing something to remedy our miserable situation. For primitive humans, this leads to the development of systems of flattery and appeasing gods - the invention of magical ceremonies that evolve into religious rites. These are clumsy, yet they have power because they bolster the confidence of those who believe in them. This confidence is the beginning of scientific faith.

Out of these primitive magical and religious systems come better methods for controlling circumstances. From magic to science is a long journey, but our knowledge of man's evolution can trace every step of the way. Nor does science altogether eliminate magic. It does get rid of the superstitions of primitive magical systems. However, even though the theory behind them was erroneous, they were successful.

The evolution of humanity and development is the work of the One Ego in Tiphareth. It is not the work of the personality. To a certain point, every human being is an operation conducted by the Ego. This operation, for any person, covers a long series of incarnations. Eventually, it brings the person to a stage of unfoldment where they can recognize what's happening. At first, this is only a glimpse. Their feelings and sensations often contradict what their intellect, in its highest activities, dimly and partially perceives.

As understanding grows, we realize that our personal development responds to something above the individual level. The real worker is the One Ego, represented by the six-pointed star in the Hermit's lantern or the charioteer in Key 7. The charioteer stands for the Son and the Divine Soul. It is a sense the central figure in the Tarot Keys stands for the One Ego. We may think of the unfoldment of personality as brought about by the cyclic manifestations of the Life-power pictured by the Wheel of Fortune or the consequence of the law that all things below the human level are shaped by human subconsciousness, as shown in Key 8.

The Tarot repeats one truth from twenty-two points of view, to which we add ten Sephiroth. The Life-power works on every human personality until it becomes a perfected instrument. The practices of occultism aim to clear channels through which the influence from Kether flows down into embodiment represented by Malkuth, the physical body's seat.

CHAPTER 5

7th Path of Hod

The Hidden Intelligence

The 7th Path is the Hidden Intelligence (Sekhel Nistar). It is the splendor that illuminates all intellectual powers that is visible to the mind's eye and contemplation of faith.

ה-נתיב	ה-שביעי	נקרא	שכל
The Path	7th	is called	Intelligence
נסתר	ו-נקרא	כן	מפני
hidden	&	so	because
latent	called		
שהוא	זוהר	מזהיר	ל-כל
that is	Zohar	bright	to all
	radiant	shining	For all
	Splendor		
ה-כחות	ה-שכליים	ה-נראים	ב-עין
the Power(s)	Intellectual	the visible	eye
Force(s)	Rational	apparent, seen	
ה-שכל	ו-ב-רעיון	ה-אמונה	
The mind	and-of-thought	the Faith	
	imagination		
	contemplation		

The 7th Path is called the Hidden Intelligence because it is the splendor shining on all intellectual virtues, which are perceived by the eyes of our reason and by the contemplation of our faith. It is called "hidden" because it is not understood but through the Intelligences of the Measures [Sephiroth]. It is distinguished from the first path because it is incomprehensible, while this one is comprehensible. Hence, it is called the "path of intellectual entities."

7th Path of Netzach

The seventh path of wisdom is the Netzach (נצח), Victory. This is the Sphere of Venus and the seat of the desire nature. It is energized by the influence proceeding downward from the fourth Sephirah through the path of Kaph (כ). This is combined with the influence from Tiphareth, descending through the path of Nun (נ). The Tree of Life color scheme shows the seventh Sephirah is green, a mixture of Chesed's blue with the yellow of Tiphareth.

Netzach is the diametrical opposite of Geburah, the Sphere of Mars. In mythology, the story of the secret love of Venus and Mars indicates this secret relationship between will and desire. Behind this myth is the idea that volition and action (Mars) are inseparable from the Venusian image-making power expressed in desire.

Netzach is at the base of the Pillar of Mercy or Wisdom, receiving the influence which flows first from Chokmah into Chesed through the path of Vav (ו). The consequence is the comprehension pictured by Key 10, which represents something seen by the mind's eye, but invisible to the eyes of the body.

The seventh path of wisdom is called Occult or Hidden Intelligence, *Sekhel Nistar* (שכל נסתר). It is from the root word, *sah.tar* (סתר), *to hide, veil, cover, conceal,* and *secret.* The powers of this path are hidden from the eye of sense.

The seventh path is "splendor that illuminates all intellectual powers that is visible to the mind's eye and contemplation of faith." Intellectual powers are *ha-kachoth ha-saykelem* (השכלים הכחות), and the second word, the plural of sekhel (שכל), we translate as "intelligence." It suggests that all the powers of consciousness are concentrated in the seventh path.

Why, in this path, is the emphasis on veiling or concealment? First, consider how desire manifests in human consciousness. When we desire something, we want it, which means we lack whatever we want. To the eye of sense, there is no visible evidence that we possess what we desire. Instead, external conditions' form and shape indicate something is missing.

The whole of creation is mental. It condenses the invisible, intangible powers of the mind into visible, tangible things. The physical plane is a projection of Life-power through mental images. So the eye of understanding and the thought of faith see our desires as something rising into our consciousness because the Life-power makes them rise. After all, desires are intimations of what is already prepared for us.

Thus the Lord answers before we call (Isaiah 65:24). Human desire is the agency whereby the Life-power brings into expression those activities which carry the creative process beyond the general averages, which are the limits of manifestation at subhuman levels.

Human personality is an instrument designed by the Life-power to fulfill its cosmic purpose. Human desire, and the forms of mental imagery which clothe those desires, demonstrate that cosmic order is a successful process. Our desires are intuitive perceptions that what we want is already ours. Hence the scientific way to become witnesses to the actual, external embodiment of what we want is, as Jesus said, to believe we have already received what we desire.

This is the thought or contemplation of faith - not blind or resting on authority. Every human achievement begins with faith. They who succeed are those who perceive with the eye of understanding that what they want is already an assured part of the cosmic order. They ground their faith in their knowledge of things as they are.

These people are in the minority at any given period of history. They take for their basis of expectation what is pictured in Key 10. They have a better vision of the cosmic order.

Their comprehension of the possibilities in humanity and their environment is more perceptive than most. Humans feel the desire to fly. They have an intuitive perception that we can fly. It begins with fantasies like the Magic Carpet's story, but ultimately it finds realization in our great airplanes. The airplane was just as possible two thousand years ago as now. The Wright brothers completed the mental image to which many predecessors had contributed. They saw it with the inner eye, penetrating the nature of things. The Wright's rational, scientific faith sustained them through all failures and discouragement until they achieved the actual flight at Kitty Hawk.

In practical occultism, we apply the same principle to human personality. We refuse to adopt the widespread view that human

77

nature cannot be changed. On the contrary, we see ourselves as participants in a continuing evolution. We live in a fortunate period because the various science branches have accumulated sufficient evidence to make it possible.

This faith has worked "miracles" for millenniums. Finally, some people put their faith to the test of an actual trial. It is far easier to build confidence because so many facts support it.

The Latin commentary on the seventh path says, "It is called "hidden" because it is not understood but through the Sephiroth's Intelligences. It is distinguished from the first path because one is incomprehensible, while this one is comprehensible. It is called the "path of intellectual entities."

Self-conscious knowledge is combined with intuitive realization. There is nothing in the surface appearances, which are based on our intellectual reckonings, enabling us to see with the eye of understanding and think with the thought of faith. We must be taught from within.

From the seventh Sephirah, three paths proceed. Two serve to carry its influence to Sephiroth, already energized. The third is the channel, which begins the actual operation of the tenth Sephirah.

The first path from Netzach is Peh (פ), illustrated by Key 16. This symbolizes the overthrow of "common sense" by spiritual intuition. It also stands for the Mars force active in Geburah and finds expression in the activities pictured by the Emperor (Aries) and Death (Scorpio). This force works in our brains to give us a higher vision **into** see things instead of looking at them. The force used in reproduction and the power enables us to form new patterns of circumstance. At its highest level, this is what humans use to bring into existence a new species of person, mentally and physically, beyond the limitations of nature-evolved homo sapiens.

This path of the letter Peh (פ) ends in the eighth Sephirah, Hod. The beginning of what is pictured by Key 16 is in our desires. We want to be more than we seem to be. We want to transcend our limitations. Sooner or later, this desire upsets the false knowledge symbolized by the Tower. It prepares us for the awakening, which shows the folly and the unreality of our supposed independence and isolation. When genuinely awakened from the dream of common sense, we begin to realize our glorious destiny.

The second path proceeding from Netzach is Tzaddi, associated with meditation. Meditation carries the thought of faith into our subconsciousness, where it begins to influence the Vital Soul activities. In practical occultism, *meditation is employed to evolve the etheric pattern of the new creature.* The new organism results from the desire for a new function. We want to be more than we seem to be. Therefore, we must dwell on our image of the new creature. Meditation transfers that image to the field of the Vital Soul or automatic consciousness. Then subconsciousness proceeds to set in motion the activities that manifest the new creature. Our conscious part of this is to meditate on the image, and this image gets more apparent as we meditate.

Path of Qoph - ק

The third path from Netzach is Qoph. This path begins the tenth Sephirah operation and is connected to our physical body. During sleep, the desires we formulate are impressed with the cell structure. Moreover, when we follow the technique explained in *Seven Steps in Practical Occultism* concerning the powers of subconsciousness, we use the forces symbolized by Key 18.

The Whole or Perfect Intelligence

The 8th Path is called the Whole or Perfect Intelligence (Sekhel Shalom). It is the Original Plan. There is no root where it can dwell except in the chamber of Gedulah (Greatness), from which its essence emanates.

שכל	נקרא	השמיני	ה-נתיב
Intelligence	is called	8	The Path

מפני	כן	ונקרא	שלם
because	so	& called	whole complete

	ה-קדמות	תכונת	שהוא
	Antiquity	attribute	It is
	original	plan	
	Primordial		

שורש	לו	אין	אשר
root	to it	no	There
origin		not	

אם	כי	בו	ל-ה-תיישב
except	because	to it	to sit, dwell

מעצם	ה-נאצלים	ה-גדולה	ב-חדרי
	Atzileem	Gedulah	room
essence	Emanation	greatness	bridal chamber

Latin Commentary

The 8th Path is called the Absolute and Perfect Intelligence because it is the primary organization; it does not have roots that are adhering unless in the most internal parts of the Sephira, which is called "Magnificence," and it stems out from its very essence. Hence, it is called the "Path of things living in water."

The 8th Path of Hod

The eighth path of wisdom, corresponding to the eighth Sephirah, Hod, is called the Perfect Intelligence *sekhel shalom* (שכל שלם). The adjective *shalom* (שלם) means "complete, finished, whole, sound, and healthy.

Full refers to completeness in number, measure, and weight. The 8th Path indicates a kind of consciousness that brings forms to completion by applying mathematical principles to accurate measurement.

Because humans can measure our form of existence, which makes possible the completion of the Life-power's other modes of expression, we can arrange our environment's elements in various kinds of order not spontaneously provided by nature. Humanity is charged with finishing the Great Work. Because we can rearrange the forms composing our mental, emotional, and physical existence, we may cultivate our personality as we cultivate plants and modify animals. By such self-cultivation, we may advance beyond the natural human limits and become a member of a new species.

This path is related to our future in the Pattern on the Trestleboard. Thus the sentence assigned to it begins, "I look forward with confidence." The three Sephiroth, which constitute the Pillar of Severity or Strength, all have to do with this prospective, or future, view of the Life-power's activities.

Binah is the Life-power's awareness of the logical consequences of what it knows itself to be – Chokmah.

Geburah is the seat of volition. Volition is concerned with applying power to change circumstances that are not yet manifested and lie in the future.

As the seat of intellect, Hod is chiefly concerned with the self-conscious process of formulating plans that shall transform desires into actualities.

Thus Hod is the Sphere of Mercury and is symbolized by the Magician. This Key shows a man applying power drawn from above to the garden below. On his table are the implements which he arranges in various patterns. At his feet are flowers. The plants' reproductive organs are the forerunners of fruits that are to come. Thus Key 1 (Beth, joining Kether to Binah) has a definite suggestion of activity aimed at results which are, according to our time-concept, in the future.

Pillar of Severity

Binah, Geburah and Hod

Three Sephiroth correspond to the black pillar on the north or left side of the Tree of Life. This pillar is marked with Beth (ב), the path leading from the Kether to Binah. Also, it's the first letter of Binah (בינה).

Pillar of Mildness or Mercy

Chokmah, Chesed and Netzach

In contrast, the white pillar is marked with the Yod (י), the special letter of Chokmah. The path of Yod leads from Chesed to Tiphareth. The symbolism of Key 9 shows an old man, representing experience, and wearing a gray garment, the hue of Chokmah in the Tree of Life color scale.

The white pillar is the manifest pillar. Its three Sephiroth (Chokmah, Chesed, and Netzach) relate to our time concept of the past. As soon as we become aware of anything, it's in the past. In a sense, it was there before we knew it. As soon as we know it, the knowledge belongs to our personal history. The *known* is the past. The unknown is the future, Chokmah, Wisdom, is the Life-power's awareness of what it always was. Chesed, Mercy, is aware that it was always beneficent and always able to supply everything necessary for manifestation. Netzach is related to desire. *When a desire rises in our minds, it is founded on a possibility or potentiality, which was already present before the unique form taken by the desire took mental shape.*

Be sure you make yourself familiar with these ideas. It may take additional study, but many practical consequences follow. First, the past manifests as Ecclesiastes 3:15 says, "That which has been is now."

When the intuitive power of Neshamah, the Divine Soul seated in Binah, comes into operation in human personality, it always deals with what is to come. Its highest manifestations are from the seer's foresight, which discerns the shape of things before those things become actualities.

The fifth Sephirah, Geburah, is called Pachad, Fear. Nobody dreads the past. It is the unknown future that inspires our terrors. Finally, the Perfect Splendor of the creative process is also in the future. We anticipate perfection, but we have not yet experienced it.

All this relates to humanity's ordinary time concept. In the higher order of knowing, Ecclesiastes says, "That which has been, is now," but it is equally right to declare, "That which is to be, has already been." This higher order of knowing, the consciousness of eternal life, lifts us out of the illusory time concept of past, present, and future. It makes our future as real as the past.

The potencies were always there. Every advance toward greater perfection is the development and unveiling of the Life-power. Hence all valid magical processes assume the objective to be reached has, so to say, already happened. They affirm the existing reality of conditions and circumstances which do not yet appear to the eye of sense. However, magicians do not force the future into a shape conformable to what they want. Like the Magician in the Tarot, he is instead a witness rather than an actor.

85

Here is a touchstone that will enable you to detect the error in all systems of "black magic." This applies to the older systems that seek to compel spirits "good and evil" to do the operator's bidding. Much relatively modern "magical practice," such as in some form of applied psychology, "advanced thought, and mental science," are tinged with the same fundamental falsehood. Whenever an ignorant religionist presumes to tell God what to do and calls this ridiculous endeavor to interfere with the cosmic order "prayer," this error is present. They who indulge themselves in vain repetitions of affirmations, thinking to be heard and answered because of their much speaking, do likewise. *Those who waste their time trying to impose personal will on people and circumstances are equally mistaken.*

Thus our text says of The Perfect Intelligence, "There is no root where it can dwell, except in the chamber of Gedulah (Greatness) from which its essence emanates." Gedulah, or Chesed, is the Life-power's unfailing beneficence. In one sense, it is Providence. The right affirmation needs no vain repetitions. It is the declaration that the desire for the perfection of things to come is provided for already. Life-power's loving provision for our every need is the root of all future blessings. It is not God or nature that we must force into bringing to pass what we want. *Instead, is it our perception that we must clarify.* True, we must make clear patterns, but we understand that these patterns are shown to us when we progress on the occult path. They are not our personal productions. They are gifts from above and from within.

Path of Mem מ

Thus the path that sets the eighth Sephirah into activity is Mem, through which the real willpower flows into Hod from Geburah. It is the path of the Hanged Man, symbolizing the consciousness that *I do nothing of myself.* Magical training aims to awaken the knowledge that good is inevitable and the best is to be confidently expected. This training calls for the self-surrender pictured by Key 12.

Path of Ayin ע

The path of Ayin (ע) connects Tiphareth to Hod, symbolized by Key 15. Our opportunities often make their first appearance as adversities. When we become aware of present limitations and feel bondage, closer scrutiny of the antagonistic situation reveals a reasonable procedure.

The *Confessio* says, "Even in the same place where there breaks forth a new disease, nature discovers a remedy against the same." Every evil is a mask concealing a positive good. Every appearance of imperfection hides the possibility of some fresh manifestation of the Eternal Splendor. The Adversary is the Redeemer who saves us by teaching us the rules of the game of life.

Thus the eighth path is our growing intellectual awareness of the perfection of the cosmic order. The power at work in it is the power of concentration, operating in the field of our self-conscious awareness.

Two Sephiroth directly influencing the eighth is the fifth path (Geburah) and the sixth (Tiphareth). The influence of Geburah descends through the path of Mem. The power of Tiphareth enters Hod through the path of Ayin. In the Tree of Life color scale, Hod is orange. It is the mixture of the red of Geburah with the yellow of Tiphareth. It is also the color complementary to the blue of Chesed, just as the green of Netzach is complementary to the red of the fifth Sephirah.

The life force in Chokmah, the Divine Soul in Binah, memory in Chesed, and volition in Geburah is above the Ego in Tiphareth. Below the One Ego are the desire nature in Netzach, the intellect in Hod, the Vital Soul in Yesod, and the physical body in Malkuth.

Through the Ego, the willpower derived from Geburah flows through Lamed and passes down to the desire-nature by Nun's channel. Through the Ego, the Life-power's eternal recollection of its beneficence flows through the channel of Yod and then through Ayin to Hod. Desire (Netzach) is complementary to will (Geburah). Intellect (Hod) is complementary to memory (Chesed). Consider this with a diagram of the Tree of Life before you.

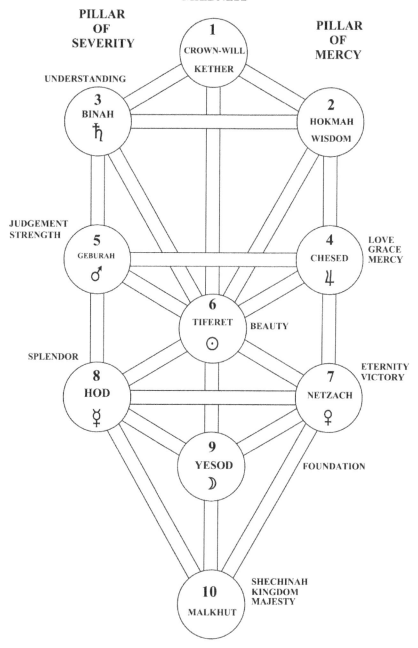

PILLAR
OF
MILDNESS

PILLAR
OF
SEVERITY

PILLAR
OF
MERCY

1
CROWN-WILL
KETHER

UNDERSTANDING

3
BINAH
♄

2
HOKMAH
WISDOM

JUDGEMENT
STRENGTH

5
GEBURAH
♂

4
CHESED
♃

LOVE
GRACE
MERCY

6
TIFERET
☉

BEAUTY

SPLENDOR

ETERNITY
VICTORY

8
HOD
☿

7
NETZACH
♀

9
YESOD
☽

FOUNDATION

SHECHINAH
KINGDOM
MAJESTY

10
MALKHUT

Descending from the Perfect Intelligence are Resh (ר) and Shin (ש). Resh carries the patterns arranged by intellectual activity (Hod) to the Vital Soul level (Yesod). In Key 19, the sun at the top stands for the eighth Sephirah. The Sphere of Mercury is to be distinguished from the planet Mercury. Our day star is a concentration of the Life-power's self-conscious energy. That self-conscious energy is the Mercury of the Sages, concentrated in the One Ego in Tiphareth.

Similarly, the One Ego (the Mercury of the Sages) is also the Sphere of the Sun. Consequently, the sixth Sephirah has a yellow color attributed to Beth's path (Mercury), while the Hod has an orange hue attributed to Resh and the Sun.

Following this clue, you can see that Chesed, the Sphere of Jupiter, is really the Moon. Hence, it is blue of the path of Gimel. Similarly, Yesod (Sphere of the Moon) is identified as Jupiter by the violet color, attributed to the Path of Kaph. Among the Sephiroth, Chesed stands for the vast reservoir of power associated with the Moon, Tiphareth for the repository of the Mercurial power, Hod for a concentration of the cosmic solar force, and Yesod for a concentration of Jupiterian power. Among the Sephiroth, only Binah (the Sphere of Saturn), Geburah (Mars), and Netzach (Venus) have the colors that are assigned to the corresponding planets. Thus Saturn, Mars, and Venus operate in and through their types of cosmic energy. However, the Sun works through the activity of Mercury, and Mercury through the Sun's operation. Jupiter operates through the cosmic concentration of lunar force in Chesed and the Moon through the vast reservoir of Jupiter's power in Yesod.

This may be a little premature. It is by no means the whole story. Nevertheless, we include it to alert students on the track of a practical secret that has never before been so plainly stated.

Path of Shin - שׁ

The path of Shin proceeds from Hod to Malkuth. It carries the patterns of the intellectual activity of Perfect Intelligence down to the physical plane. This is the "resurrection" of the spiritual body, the formation of the new creature. It is the incarnation of the human who is beyond the limitations of the ordinary genus homo. Thus the path of Shin balances that of Qoph (ק) and is of the same length,

Our next chapter will complete our explanation of the paths of Yesod and Malkuth.

CHAPTER 6

9th Path of Yesod

The Pure Intelligence

The 9th Path is the Pure Intelligence (Sekhel Tahor). It purifies the Sephiroth (numbers). It tests the law and repairs the glowing pattern (images). They are unified without any curtailment or separation.

שכל	נקרא	ה-תשיעי	ה-נתיב
Intelligence	is called	ninth	The Path

לפי	כן	ו-נקרא	טהור
because	so	& called	pure

ו-מבחין	את ה-ספירות	מטהר	שהוא
& test	Sephiroth	purifier	It is
	numbering	purifies	

ו-תוכן	תבניתם	גזירת	ו-מבהיק
& design	pattern	law	glowing

מבלי	מיוחדות	שהן	אחדותם
without	unity	to	their unity
		be hot	oneness

		ו-פירוד	קצוץ
		separate	chopped
			curtailment

Latin Commentary

The 9th Path is called the Pure Intelligence because it purifies the Sephiroth, and it approves and corrects the destruction of their appearance. It establishes the Unity of the things that are united to it with no amputation or division. It is said to be the "path of purification of things."

Yesod – Foundation

The Ninth path of wisdom is Yesod (יסוד), *Foundation*. Yesod also means *essential*, *source*, *root,* and *origin*. The Tree of Life is rooted in Kether. Yesod is the foundation for Malkuth, the tenth Sephirah, the sphere of sensation and embodiment.

Nefesh

Yesod is the seat of the Vital Soul, Nefesh (נפש). This Nefesh is latent in the mineral kingdom, where the substratum of consciousness maintains the consistency of the laws of "matter" that scientific research reveals. In the vegetable kingdom, Nefesh is made more manifest and alive because plant structures have the power of reproduction, which is the main characteristic of organic substances. In the animal kingdom, the Nefesh manifests the life-power potencies on an ascending scale of bodies, culminating in the human organism's production. Our bodies, responding to the drive of Nefesh, have undergone various changes. These "waves" of human evolution are the root races and sub-races concerning which we hear much, which is false and foolish from writers of Theosophical literature. Yet, the idea set forth by H.P.B. is correct and is not a supposition. The survivors of earlier forms of human development live on this planet today, and the remains of the earliest human beings, along with traces of their arts and modes of life, are also among us.

One neo-Theosophical dogma proposes a new race of human beings is evolving, which differs from humanity as Caucasians differ from Australian aborigines. Some proponents of this theory read that America is the scene of the development of the new race. Others say Southern California will be the locality where the first members of the new order of human beings will appear.

Western School does not accept this theory. Instead, it holds that the biological development of man has reached its term. Yet, it denies the materialistic view that ordinary homo sapiens cannot further evolve.

Ageless Wisdom teaches that further evolution is possible due to our efforts. The primary motive power is the reproductive force resident in the Vital Soul, which manifests itself in the building and modifying bodies.

This evolution is not purely biological or genetic. It is conscious evolution in which the person is an active participant, knowing what is being accomplished. We know our goal and intend that it shall be achieved. We deliberately adopt ways of thought and action that make us a member of what Judge Troward calls the Fifth Kingdom. The historical record shows many persons whose bodies represent earlier waves of evolutionary development have succeeded in the Great Work. A human's skin may be black, brown, yellow, or red. They may be of any race. If they learn what to do and do what they learn, they will become members of the Fifth Kingdom. Though their outward physical body will remain what it was before they began their practice, they will have become a member of a new species.

Consider the letters of Nefesh (נפש). It begins with Nun (נ),
attributed to Scorpio and the reproductive organs. Peh (פ) is the
Mars force. Shin (ש) represents spiritual fire.

Trace these letters on the diagram of the Tree of Life. Nun is the
link between the One Ego and the desire nature. Ageless Wisdom
declares that those who enter the Fifth Kingdom are the ones who
desire to do so, being urged to entertain that desire by the influence
flowing from the Ego into the desire nature. Additionally, physical
death awakens us to the point where we desire to be free from
bondage to death.

Peh (פ), the second letter, is the link between Netzach (desire) and
Hod (Intellect). Before the desire for release from death can be
fulfilled, many errors must be overcome. The mistaken supposition
that every human is an autonomous, self-acting creature must be
erased from consciousness. The assumption that immortality is a
postmortem state, happy or painful, according to a religious creed
or rites, must be completely eliminated. After these errors are
eliminated, it becomes possible to make more perfect patterns.
These plans are scientific. The new creature is born into the fifth
kingdom from practice.

At this stage of the Great Work, one participates as a witness
instead of an actor. The result is a definite modification of the
physical organism. They know the lightning flash in Key 16, the
angel in Key 20, and the reaper in Key 13 are super-personal
powers. The One Ego's power in Tiphareth brings everyone that
enters the Fifth Kingdom into that higher order of knowledge,
action, and life. This runs like a golden thread through the New
Testament parables. It is all humanity's destiny to eventually enter

the Fifth Kingdom, but they do not come all at once, nor do they join by biological evolution. "Flesh and blood do not inherit the Kingdom." The One Ego is the Good Shepherd of the parables, and none of the sheep, the personal human expressions, is lost forever. It can take many incarnations to bring a personality to the point where it can participate in its conscious evolution. Nevertheless, the School of Ageless Wisdom declares it will arrive eventually.

The Path of Samekh ס

On the Tree of Life, three paths lead to Yesod from the Sephiroth above. They are the paths of Samekh, Tzaddi, and Resh. The path of Samekh is illustrated by Key 14. It shows the One Ego as the Holy Guardian Angel, tempering and modifying the Vital Soul and communicating the direct influence from Tiphareth. The pool at the angel's feet is a symbol of Yesod. The lion symbolizes the twenty-sixth path Ayin (ע), and the eagle stands for the twenty-fifth path of the letter Nun (נ).

The Path of Tzaddi צ

The path of Tzaddi corresponds to meditation. The nude woman kneeling in Key 17 symbolizes the One Ego because the Ego, usually called the Son, is androgyne. Meditation is a function of the One Ego, which raises the powers of the automatic consciousness in Yesod to the conscious level, symbolized by the pool. Therefore, those who seek to enter the Fifth Kingdom must meditate. However much it may seem to us that meditation is a personal activity, we discover that we are being contemplated when we succeed in meditation.

96

The Path of Resh ר

The path of Resh (ר) is pictured by Key 19, the Sun. It represents the early stages of humanity's awareness of becoming a new creature. It portrays something occurring on conscious and subconscious levels. The two children symbolize self and subconsciousness. The sun behind them is like the angel of Key 14. They are individual embodiments of "solar consciousness." Their dance in a fairy ring manifests the One Ego's personal conscious energy in Tiphareth, symbolized by the day star with a human face.

Pure Intelligence

The ninth path of Yesod is called *Sekhel Tahor* (שכל טהור), the Pure Intelligence. The adjective *tahor* means *clean*. The name dismisses all false notions of the stigma of impurity on the reproductive power fundamental for evolution. False dogmas of religion are partly responsible for these errors. The average person's childhood bad conditioning and preoccupation with sense experience contribute their share to this grave misunderstanding. There is no more impurity in animal and human reproduction processes than in plants' flowering. It is a gross error to suppose that entry into the Fifth Kingdom requires repudiation of the human body's normal function. Practical occultist achievements are not brought about by painful asceticism.

On the contrary, the adepts make themselves members of the Fifth Kingdom by utilizing the reproductive power surplus of energy. The Great Work brings the occultist to the Fifth Kingdom. A magician is like an engineer who devises and erects dams to hold back floodwaters and conserve them in reservoirs, from which they are carried through a system of canals and irrigation ditches. All sound and workable occult practices have, for their object, the intelligent use, never the suppression, of the reproductive forces.

The word *tahor* (טהור) tells us as much. Its first letter is Teth (ט), illustrated by a woman taming a lion in Key 8. She leads with a wreath of roses that represent desire. The lion is a symbol of the force concentrated in Yesod. He is tamed, not killed.

The second letter is Heh (ה) and is pictured by the Emperor, a type of fatherhood. His authority (look closely at that word) is the immediate consequence of his fathering those he rules. The Emperor is related to man's power of directing the course of circumstance through the exercise of foresight. Engineers build dams and canals utilizing the same ability to tame the floodwaters. The mental functions pictured by the Emperor have to do with the highest manifestations of the ninth path of wisdom. These mental powers are closely related to the higher functions of the reproductive organs.

The third letter is Vav (ו), pictured by the Hierophant. Vav is numerical six and therefore associated with the sixth Sephirah, Tiphareth. The Hierophant represents the One Self, which spoke through Jesus when he said: "Before Abraham was, I am." It is the teacher and guide of humanity. It is the instructor of the principles of eternal truth. The secret wisdom it reveals and ever re-veils concerns the direction of the forces concentrated in Yesod. The roes and lilies on the kneeling ministers' vestments symbolize reproductive activity, as are the flowers in the magician's garden in Key 1.

The last letter of *tahoor* is Resh (ר). It is the path leading from Hod to Yesod. What we have said previously will enable you to understand how it applies to the idea of purification.

The text says that Pure Intelligence purifies the essence of the Sephiroth. The Nefesh in Yesod acts like a filter or a distilling apparatus. In our human personality, the Vital Soul is the active agency of subconsciousness. The Sphere of the Moon, typified as the High Priestess, is at work in shaping, maintaining, and transforming our bodies. The Vital Soul's subconscious level carries on all heredity operations. These do not include the transmission from generation to generation of a single personal incarnation's acquired characteristics and habits. It is only the essence of the Sephiroth, concentrated in Yesod. The accidental details of our many own lives are filtered out.

Images - תבנית

By the functions of this ninth path, the fitness of every human personality is tested and tried. The text says of Pure Intelligence, "It tests the law and repairs the pattern (images)" of the Sephiroth. The word "images" is *Tav.neet* (תבנית), meaning "form, model, pattern." Deep in subconsciousness are the patterns for every cell and every organ of our bodies. During gestation, physical body development is interfered with, like crystals' growth is determined by their environment. Yet, the fundamental types are always present in subconsciousness. When the One Ego selects personalities for entry into the Fifth Kingdom, they are called and chosen whose organisms are ready for the work.

Yesod's powers are sent down into the tenth Sephirah through a single path. Yesod is the only Sephirah that pours the descending influence through a single channel into a single Sephirah - the path Tav, illustrated by Key 21.

In this connection, we see cosmic consciousness pictured by Key 21, which is the agency whereby the power of Yesod enters the field of sensation and physical embodiment (Malkuth). What makes a flower grow, or a mother's body develop during gestation, is the universal life, acting through the plant or animal organism. In a sense, everything is conceived by the Holy Spirit. What the angel Gabriel said to Mary is true of all living organisms that bring forth new generations: "The Holy Spirit will come over you, and the power of the Most High will overshadow you." This miracle is not extraordinary. The explicit statement of an eternal law is always at work. There may have been a unique and unusual operation of this law in the conception and birth of Jesus. To deny it is to maintain the presumptuous opinion that we know all there is to know how the Life-power provides itself with physical vehicles. To affirm it as being a fact, like any other fact of history, is to say too much. Whether or not one accepts the Virgin Birth story as a myth or history can only be a belief at this distance from the event. However, this belief makes Jesus the Great Exception instead of the Great Example. This bodybuilding process is the Spirit's work so that every mother is overshadowed by the Most High. The inner knowledge of every sensitive mother will testify to this.

Tav corresponds to the "temple of holiness in the midst." Recall that within and above are synonymous. Therefore, we know that the influence of Tav's path leading from Yesod to Malkuth is centered on human life. The Holy Spirit over-shadows because it is a power transcending personality limitations. We may compare it to the waves from a broadcasting station, far more powerful than the weak current in a receiving set. The broadcasting station influences every receiver tuned to the station while being active within each receiver. The station determines what comes out of the receiver, just as the cosmic life pictured by Key 21 determines the lives of the central Ego's innumerable personalities.

Saturn, the Adversary

Until we understand it, this determining influence is a mask of antagonism. For the ordinary human being, the world is an enemy, along with the flesh and the devil. Key 21 is associated with Saturn, which rules Capricorn, symbolized by Key 15, the Devil. The same active principle operates through Key 15, 21, and Binah. Thus, Tav's path and Binah's color are deep indigo, though the third Sephirah is commonly tinted black.

Paths of Qoph and Shin

Two other paths lead down to Malkuth from above. From Netzach descends the path of Qoph (ק), corresponding to the Corporeal Intelligence, which "marks out the forms of all bodies which are incorporated under every revolution of the zodiac." From Hod descends the path of Shin (ש), corresponding to Perpetual Intelligence, "It regulates all the cyclic forces that form the revolutions of the zodiac." The path of Qoph and Key 18 corresponds to evolution. Shin has to do with the future, and Key 20 symbolizes the completion of the evolutionary cycle, hence its title, Judgment.

The Scintillating Intelligence

The 10th Path is Scintillating Intelligence (Sekhel mit.Notz.etz). It is exalted and sits on the throne of Binah (Understanding). It illuminates the splendor of all the lights and causes an influx of increase from the Prince of Face.

ה-נתיב	ה-עשירי	נקרא	שכל
The Path	tenth	is called	Consciousness

מתנוצץ	ו-נקרא	כן	שהוא
Shining Scintillating	& called	so	that is

מפני	מתעלה	ו-יושב	על
because	exalted - העלה	& sits	on

כסא	ה-בינה	ו-מאיר	ב-זוהר
seat	*Binah*	illuminate	*Zohar*
throne - כס	Understanding		splendor

ה-מאורות	כולם	ו-משפיע	שפע
lights	everyone	influx	influx
illumination		influence	abundance

ריבוי	ל-שר	ה-פונים	
increase	Prince	the face	
multiply		appearance	

Latin Commentary

The 10th Path is called the Sparkling Intelligence because it has been exalted above every individual and is located on the throne of Binah. It emits the flare of all lights and acts so that it gives license to the "head of images." It is the "Path of the variety of things."

Malkuth, the 10th Path

The tenth path of wisdom is the tenth Sephirah, *Malkuth* (מלכות), Kingdom. This is the physical world, the seat of sensation, and *guph* (גוף), the physical body. It is also the Sphere of the Elements, called *Cholom Yesodoth* (חלם יסודות), "The Breaker of the Foundations," because it is the field in which the fundamental unity of cosmic substance appears to be broken up into the four classifications, designated as Fire, Water, Air, and Earth.

On the Tree of Life, the circle of Malkuth is divided into four segments.

The top is citrine, a mixture of Netzach's green and Hod's orange. The citrine segment corresponds to Air.

The right part is olive or slate, a blend of Netzach's green and Yesod's violet. The olive segment corresponds to Water.

The left segment is russet. It is a mixture of orange (Hod) and violet (Yesod). The russet segment corresponds to Fire.

At the bottom is a section colored black, or deep indigo, produced by the mixture of the secondary colors, green, orange, and violet. This segment corresponds to the element of Earth.

The numeral value of *Malkuth* (מלכות) is 496. The sum of numbers from 0 to 31 or the extension of 31 is 496. Now, 31 is the value of the divine name El (אל), Strength, assigned to the fourth Sephirah. It is also the number of *lo* (לא), meaning NOT or NO-THING. Here is a reminder that the Kingdom is the full manifestation of that Divine Strength, itself *lo* (לא), NO-THING.

496 is the third perfect number, the two preceding 6 and 28 (see Appendix 4). Thus it is a numeral symbol for the perfect manifestation of Life-power. Malkuth is the final Sephirah of the series, poured, as Tree of Life shows, from the influences descending from the thirty-one paths above. This is numerically indicated because 496 is the extension of 31.

Kallah – Bride

Consequently, one of the names for Malkuth is Kallah (כלה), the Bride. Numerically, Kallah is 55, with the extension of 10. That is to say, Malkuth is the complete expression of the powers of the ten Sephiroth.

The letters of Kallah (כלה) can be arranged to spell *ha-kal* (ה כל), "The All." This suggests Malkuth represents the sum-total of the influences shown on the Tree of Life, concentrated into the field of manifestation of Malkuth. As homo sapiens, the only world we know is the sensory experience of mental impressions of sensations received through our physical body. Sensations are the basis of human knowledge, whether that knowledge is superficial and inaccurate as of a savage or as penetrating and exact as a scientist.

Melek – King

The root of the word Malkuth (מלכות) is Melek (מלך), King, which is one of the names for Tiphareth. Thus, the 10th Sephirah's fundamental idea is the manifestation or expression of the power to rule, derived from the Ego or the Christos.

The temple of God is a house not made with hands, eternal in the heavens, and that temple is embodied in humanity. Saint Paul said, "Know you are the temple of God, and that the Spirit of God dwells in you?" (1 Corinthians 3:16)

That temple is already eternal in the heavens. The power that made the worlds, and rules everything in the universe, has its dwelling in this temple NOW. We do not have to wait until we are dead to know this. Nor do we have to do anything to establish the embodiment of the Kingdom of Spirit in our flesh.

One numerical correspondence to Malkuth (מלכות) is Leviathan
(לויתן), the great serpent of the deep. Myths say Leviathan causes
eclipses of the sun and moon by swallowing the luminaries or
throwing its folds around them. Therefore, Leviathan is the serpent
of darkness and the great devourer. It is used as a symbol for Egypt
in Psalm 74 and Isaiah 47. In these two passages, Leviathan is a
symbol of a symbol since Egypt represents the darkness of the
physical plane and the earth as the great grave that swallows
generation after generation of human bodies. Thus Leviathan is the
symbol of the physical plane, as it appears to the ignorant.

It symbolizes the Old Serpent, the cosmic antagonist closely
related to the Tiamat of Babylonian mythology. Yet this is "The
All" (הכל), and when we understand it, the dark antagonist is seen
as the perfect order or Kingdom.

Resplendent is from a root *nawtzatz* (נוצץ) to glitter, bloom, or flower. Malkuth is called the flower of the Tree. The number of *Mathanutzatz* is 656, as is Galgalim (גלגלים), whirlings or whirling motion. Galgalim is the term for the sum total of the manifestations of the cosmic forces, which have their beginning in Kether. The Path of Malkuth in any world is always a receptacle for the total forces and activities expressed by that world.

The Resplendent Intelligence *sekhel mathanatzo* (שכל מתנוצץ) is so-called "because it is exalted [above every head], and sits on the throne of Binah." Here is an explicit statement linking the ideas of Binah and Malkuth. The world we see surrounding us seems full of darkness and opacity. Yet, when we learn how to see into it, we find that it is all light and brightness. Even modern science states that the physical world manifests as scintillating energy: Aur (אור), Light, the Rosicrucian L.V.X.

We are told that if our eye is single, our body will be full of light. Yet, when we see the UNITY of the ALL, we have the single eye, the eye of the illuminated mind. Then we see the real substance of the universe is spiritual –what we experience through sensation is the real presence of the Divine Spirit, veiled by the appearances of "matter."

This is beautifully expressed in a greeting written by Fra Giovanni to a friend in the year 1513:

> "The gloom of the world is but a shadow. Behind it, yet
> within our reach, is Joy. There are radiance and glory in the

darkness. So could we but see – and to see, we have only to look. I implore you to look.

"Life is so generous a giver, but judging its gifts by their covering, we cast them away as ugly, heavy, or hard. Remove the covering, and you will find beneath it a living splendor woven of love, by wisdom, with power. Welcome it, grasp it, and touch the Angel's hand that brings it to you. Believe me, everything we call a trial, a sorrow, or a duty, that Angel's hand is there; the gift is there, and the wonder of an overshadowing Presence."

This Presence is the Resplendent Intelligence, which is exalted above every head. We know this when we follow Fra Giovanni's counsel and take the gifts life brings us. Then we look at every circumstance of our lives as a particular dealing of God with our soul. Accepting and grasping the gift is adopting a willingly receptive attitude toward all experiences and the determination to comprehend them.

Kallah

The word Kallah (כלה) sums this up. The first letter is Kaph (כ), representing comprehension, illustrated by the Wheel of Fortune. The second is Lamed (ל), illustrated by Justice and action. The last is Heh (ה), symbolized by the Emperor, whose foresight gives him authority and power over circumstance. To grasp the meaning of experience, we must take every event as a gift, having a positive value that may be comprehended and understood. Then we must act continually to make the adjustments this clear comprehension necessitates. The fruit of this is a true vision, real insight, and dependable foresight.

Follow the ancient admonition: "Relate thyself neither to the past nor the future: live out the present with a smiling heart." To be fully receptive to what occurs NOW, resolve to take it, understand it, and apply it. This is to open the single eye to the Heavenly Vision of the Spiritual Kingdom, which is eternally embodied in our flesh.

Our next chapter will deal with the eleventh and twelfth paths of wisdom. These are the paths of the letters Aleph and Beth, illustrated by Keys 0 and 1.

CHAPTER 7

11th Path of Aleph - א

Shining Consciousness

The 11th Path is the Shining or Scintillating Intelligence (Sekhel M'tzuk.tzach). It is truly the essence of the veil which arranges the sequence of the stars. It assigns the Paths their relationships. And (it) stands before the Cause of Causes.

שכל	עשר	אחד	ה-נתיב
Intelligence	10	1	The Path
מפני	כן	ו-נקרא	מצוחצח
because	rightly	& called	shining
	true		scintillating
ה-מסודר	ה-פרגוד	עצם	שהיא
the arrangement	the veil	essence	that is
the ordered	curtain	Bone	
יחס	ו-הוא	ה-מערכה	ב-סדר
assign	and it (he)	the array	in succession
attribute	*Hu* – Kether's	disposition of	sequence
	divine name	the stars	series
ה-עילות עילת	ב-פני	ל-עמוד	ה-נתנת
Cause of causes	in front, before	to stand	the paths

The 11th Path is called the Luminous Intelligence because it is the curtain placed by the disposition and order of the higher and lower paths, and it is a sort of dignity granted to it to stay in front of the Cause of Causes.

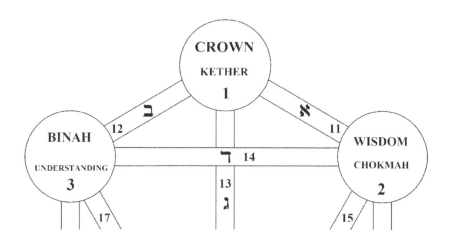

The path of Aleph (א), joining Kether to Chokmah, is called the Scintillating Intelligence *Sekhel* MeTzuchtach (שכל מצוחצח). The eleventh path is the channel for the first outpouring from Kether, the concentrated white brilliance of the Limitless Light. Finally, the Cause of Causes is a title of Kether, the Crown – the 1st Path.

The letter-name *Aleph* (אלף) is the exact reversal of the adjective *pehleh* (פלא), *wonderful*, which designates the first path of wisdom, Kether. This reversal refers to mirroring, associated with the Life-power's reflection of itself in Wisdom.

At the stage of manifestation represented by Aleph and the Fool, there are no distinguishable *things*. Therefore, that mode of consciousness may be called *consciousness of nothing*. Hence the Key corresponding to Aleph bears a zero sign.

Taken letter by letter, *Aleph* (אלף) represents the first outflow of spiritual influence (א), effecting a continual equilibration of forces in action (ל), resulting in the positive expression of the creative thought (ף) of the Universal Mind.

The first two letters of Aleph (אלף) form the divines name *El* (אל), which is assigned to the fourth Sephirah, Chesed. The word *El* (אל) meaning is *nothing* or *naught*. In the Old Testament, there are many examples of this usage. With different vowel pointing, the same two letters signify *strength*, *might*, *power*, and *God*. Here is more than a hint that God is nothing perceptible to our senses, nothing we may ever define.

Separating the letters of Aleph (אלף) into (אל ף) suggests a power that cannot be limited by any of our human ideas concerning it. El (אל) 's power manifests through speech associated with the letter Peh (פ). The combination (ף ל א) would be the *Mouth of God* or *Divine Self-expression*.

The text says the eleventh path is "truly the essence of the veil which arranges the sequence of the stars." In its outpouring, the Divine Self-expression veils its inner nature in Name and Form's illusions, producing the phenomenal universe. An ancient aphorism says the same, "The Spirit clothes itself to come down, and strips itself to go up." – The Mysteries of Magic: A Digest of the Writings of Eliphas Lévi, p. 192

The superior causes are the first three Sephiroth, Kether, Chokmah, and Binah. They are the *Three Supernals*. The seven Sephiroth following, from Chesed to Malkuth, are the *inferior causes*. Their dispositions and order are diagrammed in the Tree of Life.

In Chapter 1, we read that Adept's power and privilege corresponding to Aleph is to "behold God face to face without dying, and converse familiarly with the seven genii who command the entire celestial army." The inferior causes are the same as the seven genii, and the text ends with the statement that he who possesses this path "stands face to face with the Cause of Causes."

The letter-name Aleph (אלף) is numerically 111. This is the value of *ehben-khane* (אבן כן), the true stone. Ehben (אבן) symbolizes the union of the Father and the Son. Khane (כן) is a shorthand for Chokmah Nesethrah (חכמה נשטרה), "secret wisdom." The secret wisdom is the Qabalah. A practical occultism system leads its adepts to recognize the identity between the one human Ego, seated in Tiphareth (the Son), and the cosmic life-force seated in Chokmah (the Father).

The nature of this experience escapes verbal expression, but it is known to be a clear vision of Divine Unity. Thus it is related to the words *echad hu Elohim* (אחד הוא אלהים), "One is He, God." In this phrase, the first word refers to Chokmah, the second to Kether, and the third to Binah, so it sums up the powers of the first three Sephiroth.

The Archangels of the Planets

The seven genii are the angels of the seven Sephiroth from Binah to Yesod. They are the archangels:

Sephiroth	Sphere of	Archangel of the Planet	Hebrew
Binah	Saturn	Tzaphqiel	צפקיאל
Chesed	Jupiter	Tzadkiel	צדקיאל
Geburah	Mars	Kamael	כמאל
Tiphareth	The Sun	Michael	מיכאל
Netzach	Venus	Haniel	האניאל
Hod	Mercury	Raphael	רפאל
Yesod	The Moon	Gabriel	גבריאל

These are not separate beings flying from place to place. On the contrary, they are aspects of the ONE LIFE-POWER present everywhere. Each is a manifestation of a phase of the *single* Divine Power. Thus, all their names end with the syllable אל, El, "God."

Tzaphqiel (or Zaphkiel) [צפקיאל] is the ONE GIVER, manifesting itself as the Divine Soul, Neshamah, seated in Binah. Tzaphqiel means "Contemplation of God," and this Divine Vision of the logical consequences of what the Life-power knows itself to become when we attune ourselves to the Divine Soul.

Tzadqiel (or Zadkiel) [צדקיאל] is the ONE POWER, manifest as the Universal Memory in Chesed. The Life-power's perfect recollection of itself and all its manifestations is founded in loving kindness. Its beneficent righteousness is expressed by the word Tzadqiel, "Righteousness of God."

Kamael (כמאל) signifies "Severity of God" and is attributed to the fifth Sephirah, Geburah. It is Life-power as the force we feel within us as volition.

Michael (מיכאל) is the archangel of the Sun and Tiphareth. It designates the One Ego in Tiphareth. The name means "Like unto God."

Haniel (האניאל) is the archangel of Netzach and Venus. The name means "Grace of God," and behind it is the thought that the working of the desire nature in Netzach manifests the Divine Grace, which has already prepared for us the good gifts we desire.

Raphael (רפאל) is the archangel of the Sphere of Mercury, Hod. It designates Life-power as the active principle of Intellect, whereby things are brought to fulfillment and perfection. The name means "God the Healer."

Gabriel (גבריאל) is the archangel of the Sphere of the Moon and the automatic consciousness in Yesod. Therefore Gabriel is the angel of the Annunciation. In the New Testament, his name stands for the Life-power's manifestation in all the reproduction processes. It signifies "Strength (literally, virile or procreative force) of God."

Conforming with these celestial army genii is to *attune* oneself to their characteristic qualities. This is the power attributed to the eleventh path of wisdom because the superconsciousness experienced by the "possessor" of this path has control of the energy Ruach (רוח). In Sanskrit, it's Prana. As Swami Vivekananda said;

Ruach and Prana

"(The knowledge and control of this Prana) opens the door to almost unlimited power. Suppose, for instance, we understood the Prana perfectly and could control it. What power on earth could there be that would not be his? He would be able to move the suns and stars out of their places, to control everything in the universe, from the atoms to the biggest suns because he would control the Prana. When the Yogi becomes perfect, nothing in nature will be under his control. If he orders the gods to come, they will come at his bidding; if he asks the departed to come, they will come at his bidding. All the forces of nature will obey him as his slaves, and when the ignorant see these powers of the Yogi, they call them miracles... He who has grasped the Prana has grasped all the forces of the universe, mental or physical."

This is the "great dignity" enjoyed by a possessor of the eleventh path of wisdom. To enter into the state of superconsciousness symbolized by the Fool is to become an open, unobstructed channel for the outflow of Ruach (רוח), the Holy Spirit.

The 12th Path of Beth - ב

Glowing Intelligence

The 12th Path is Glowing Intelligence (Sekhel Bahir). It is the essence of the Great Wheel (the zodiac). It is called the Visualizer (Chaz.chaz.it). It is the source of vision of the prophets and those who see apparitions.

ה-נתיב	שנים	עשר	נקרא
The Path	2	10	is called

שכל	בוער	מפני	שהוא
Consciousness Intelligence	glowing burning	because	that is

עצם	ה-אופן	ה-גדלה	ו-נקרא
essence bone substance	The wheel	the great magnificence	& called

חזחזית	פי	מקים	מוצא
Visualizer	transitive verb	place, spot dwelling-place	source fountain
חזית seeing, prophecy			

חזיון	ה-חוזים	ב-מראה	
vision	prophets	appearance, vision mirror	

The 12th Path is called the "Transparent Intelligence" because it is the appearance of magnificence and the place from which the vision stems for those who see with apparitions. So, through it, a prophecy is obtained, and we reach the Supreme Chariot.

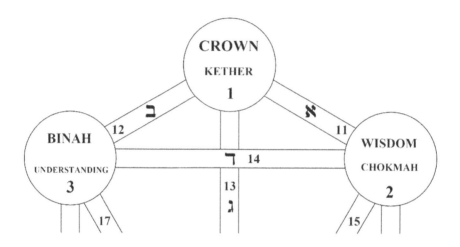

The twelfth path is Beth (ב), joining Kether to Binah is the Glowing Intelligence, *Sekhel Bahir* (שכל בוער). The twelfth path is the second channel pouring from Kether. The first channel is *shining*, which implies something that reflects light. The second channel, the Glowing Intelligence, is the outpouring of primal fire into Binah, the Divine Mother.

Rabbi Yitzchak Ginsburgh has this to say about the light of Beth.

"Just as darkness exists below light, in the sense of concealment of light from consciousness, so darkness exists above light, in the sense of the absolute consciousness above all possible revelation of light. In this world, our relation to this higher darkness is only through simple faith. In the future, we shall know this darkness just as we know light. Then the darkness will "shine" with brilliance incomparable to any known light.

"This is an even deeper understanding of the open side of the Beit [ב]; in the future, it will be simultaneously open (unknown and dark) and closed (known and light)." – *The Hebrew Letters*, p. 43

The letter-name Beth (בית) can be separated into ב and ית. Yath (ית) is the Accusative or Objective Case (the direct object of a verb). That's like pointing your finger and saying, "I'm talking to you." In thinking of Beth (בית) as Be-yath, mental activity is directed toward a specific object. The idea of action, centered on a particular objective, is clearly expressed by the symbolism of Key 1.

The power in the twelfth path comes from above and passes through the self-consciousness typified by the Magician *into* the field below. This principle, like that at work in the eleventh path, is the Limitless Light concentrated in the whirling motion of Kether.

The twelfth path is the "image (or body, or substance) of that wheeling of Gedulah which is called Chazchazith (חזחזית)." The word is probably Chaldaic, but it is derived from the same root as chaz.oth (חזות), signifying vision or revelation.

The higher and more accurate vision we designate by the term insight is the power at work in the twelfth path. A lazy, superficial, or careless observer is never gifted with insight.

One must look attentively at appearances to develop the ability to see into them. Likewise, a builder must know the ground and the quality of materials before constructing a home.

The eleventh path represents the vision of the cosmic One Self – super-consciousness. It is the link between Yekhidah and Chaiah. In the Cube of Space, the vertical coordinate connects the center of the top surface with the bottom surface. Consequently, this links self-consciousness (Above) and subconsciousness (Below). In the Tarot's symbolism, the Fool is a youthful androgyne figure, poised at the edge of great height, with a yawning abyss at his feet.

The Fool looks up. In contrast, is the Magician symbolism. His gaze and a pointing finger are directed to the garden below. As self-consciousness, he is related to the upper surface of the Cube. He is a seer and all his magical power results from a clear and penetrating vision. He symbolizes the power of Yekhidah (unique essence), descending into the subconscious field of Binah, the Sphere of Saturn, the area of limitation and specialization, in which are to be found at work the powers that produce the multiplicity of conditions and things, through the law of differentiation. The Magic of Light is the conscious direction of this law.

The Essence of the Great Wheel

The text says the 12th Path is "the essence of the Great Wheel." In the Tarot, The Wheel of Fortune is Jupiter and Chesed.

Chesed is the seat of memory. Vision requires memory. We do not really see anything until we recognize it. Yet, Chesed is at a lower level than that of the 12th Path. This indicates that a phase of the great (Gedulah) wheel is *in the first Sephirah*. Per the Qabalistic doctrine, every Sephirah contains a whole Tree of Life within itself.

The Latin text says, "it is the place, from which the vision stems out for those who see with apparitions."

Apparitions are not limited to ghosts or other phantasms. The power we are concerned with here is the power to perceive even ordinary sense appearances.

Case translated this path as "transparent." However, the Hebrew word (באיר) is used in Kircher's book, but I cannot find it in Alcalay's dictionary. Transparent is ברור. Burning or glowing is בוער.

In Sepher Yetzirah, Kaplan translates the word "glowing."

CHAPTER 8

13th Path of Gimel - ג

Unity Directing Consciousness

The 13th *Path* is the Unity Directing Intelligence (*Sekhel Man.hig Ha.Achdut*). It is the essence of Glory and truly the reward of the spiritual ones.

ה-נתיב	שלשה	עשר	נקרא
The Path	3	10	is called

שכל	מנהיג	ה-אחדות	מפני
Intelligence	leader	the unity(s)	because
	directing	uniting	

שהוא	עצם	ה-כבוד	ו-הוא
It is	essence	the glory	and it (he)
	substance		*Hu*

תשלום	אמתת	ה-רוחניים	ה-אחדים
reward	truth	Spiritual(s)	"the ones"
completion	verify, confirm		

The 13th Path is called the Inductive (Conductive in the original Case lessons) Intelligence of Unity because it is the essence of glory and perfects the truth of each spiritual thing. All the paths that unite to the Supreme Unity join themselves through this 13th Path. In fact, echad [אחד], interpreted as a number, gives 13.

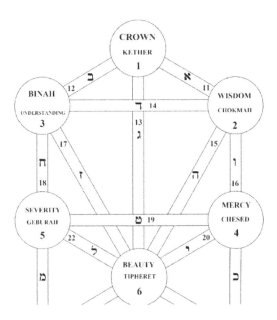

The 13th Path is Gimel (ג), joining Kether to Tiphareth and symbolized by the High Priestess. It is named the Uniting Intelligence, or Unity Directing Consciousness, *Sekhel Man.hig Ha.Achdut* (שכל מנהיג ה-אחדות), or "Leader of the Unities."

Hebrew does not use a dash "-" to separate words. It's used in these chapters to facilitate learning. The letter Heh (ה) means *the*. The last two letters Vav-Tav (ות), indicate the word is feminine plural. The root word is echad (אחד), meaning *one, single*. Therefore ha-*echudoth* literally means "the unities."

Uniting Intelligence is literally: "Driver of Unities." *Menahig* (מנהיג), a leader, is from the verb *minhag* (מנהג), to drive (as a chariot). Studying the Tree of Life and its relationships is often called "The Work of the Chariot."

13th Path of Gimel ג

In the path of Gimel, there may be movement in two directions outward and downward from above and inward and upward from below. In the paths of Aleph and Beth, the movement is always outward and downward. One does not traverse them in the reverse direction. Those who arrive at Kether are identified consciously with the Indivisible One Self, Yekhidah, and participate in its eternal outflow through the eleventh and twelfth paths.

The thirteenth path is the manifestation of the subconsciousness of Yekhidah, the cosmic One Self. The eleventh path of Aleph is the manifestation of Yekhidah's super-consciousness. The twelfth of Beth is the expression of its self-consciousness. It is the thirteenth path of Gimel where the Yekhidah's subconscious, eternal self-recollection pours into Tiphareth and brings into operation the One Ego of all humanity

This path is the essence of glory, *etzem ha-kabode* (עצם ה-כבוד). The word etzem, is 200, the number of the letter Resh (ר), attributed to the Sun. *Ha-kabode* (ה-כבוד) is 37, the same as Yekhidah (יחידה), which designates the cosmic One Self in Kether. Furthermore, ha-kabode, means weight and gravitation. Thus the Gematria of *etzem ha-kabode* (עצם ה-כבוד) indicates that the *essence of glory* is the gravitational force of the radiant energy which is concentrated in Kether. The total value of *etzem ha-kabode* is 237, which is the same as the letter-name Gimel, spelled in full (גמל מים למד) so that there is a correspondence between Gimel's letter name and the thirteenth path.

The thirteenth path also connects with the Seal of the United States, with many repetitions of the number 13. On the Seal's reverse is the symbol of an eye in a triangle, surrounded by a glory. In Latin Gematria, the words eye (*oculus*), triangle (*trygono*), and *glory (gloria)* total values 237. Note that glory is directly connected with the thirteenth path.

The number 237 is the value of the First Veil of the Absolute. En (אין), spelled in full (אלף יוד נון). The *essence of glory* is the No-Thing, the most abstract conception our minds can form concerning the nature of the ONE BEING, which is the Rootless Root of all manifestation. The No-Thing finds expression in appearance (the eye), the Three Supernals (the triangle), and radiant energy, the substance of things. Also, *kabode* (glory) is associated with gravitation or weight that holds together the world of name and form.

The power of recollection is essential in the thirteenth path. In the symbolism of the High Priestess, it is represented by her scroll inscribed with the word TORA (Law) to show the "laws of nature" are the Life-power's perfect memory of the orderly sequences of its self-expression.

Kabode – Glory

Fundamental in all life-power manifestations is electromagnetic radiant energy, called Aur (אור), by Qabalists and L.V.X. in the Western School. Einstein has devised a formula indicating the essential unity of gravitation (kabode, glory) and electromagnetism. Kabode, though its primary meaning is weight, in the Bible, it is splendor or glory as represented by the All-seeing Eye's glory on the United States Seal. This glory is a radiance shining forth from the light source.

The Latin text says, "All the paths, which unite themselves to the Supreme Unity, join themselves through this 13th path."

If we trace the Tree of Life paths in reverse order, beginning at Malkuth, *the thirteenth is the last path that leads upward.* It takes us from Tiphareth, the seat of The One Ego, back to Kether, the seat of the cosmic One Self, Yekhidah, and once we have come there, we have reached the end of the Way of Return.

The letter-name Gimel (גמל) is 73, and so is Chokmah (חכמה). Hence the High Priestess, who bears the number of Chokmah, 2, represents the lesser Chokmah or the feminine aspect of cosmic wisdom. Thus, like the Gnostic Sophia, she stands for the perfect self-recollection and self-knowledge of the One Being.

Key 2 – The High Priestess

The thirteenth path is represented by Key 2, a symbol of memory. The High Priestess's scroll, bearing the word TORA, Law, is rolled in a spiral to indicate the force concentrated in Kether is whirling energy. ROTA is Latin for a wheel. Since ROTA is a rearrangement of TORA's letters, it suggests the scroll is the Law of Rotation, symbolized by Key 10.

Key 10 corresponds to Jupiter, and in astrology, there is a close relationship between Jupiter and the Moon, which is attributed to Gimel. The Moon rules Cancer, where Jupiter is exalted. In Key 18, the Moon, corresponding to Pisces, is ruled by Jupiter. Both title and symbolism emphasize the Moon's influence. On the Tree of Life, the Sphere of the Moon is violet, the color attributed to Jupiter.

The Grade of Lesser Adept is the conscious realization that what each of us designates as "I" is the One Ego in everyone. Then it is possible to follow the Way of Return, up through the thirteenth path, to Kether. This path is not open until the adept has traversed all the paths leading upward from Tiphareth, beginning with Lamed and ending with Daleth. Only those who have attained the Grade of Magus, corresponding to Chokmah, follow the path of Gimel back to Kether. The starting point for this final advance on the Way of Return is realizing that the Son (Tiphareth) is in perfect union with the Father (Chokmah). This realization is incomplete until the adept is consciously united with the Father-life in Chokmah. When accomplished, the way opens for the supreme identification – that the One Ego in Tiphareth reflects Yekhidah in Kether.

Thus, Eliphas Levi's manuscript says the thirteenth path's possessor "reigns with all heaven and is served by all hell." In Hebrew, hell is "Sheol," and in Greek, "Hades," It is not a place of damnation and the abode of malignant spirits. On the contrary, it is the realm of shades, the astral plane, corresponding to Yesod on the Tree of Life.

To be "served by all hell" is to use the astral plane's powers well. "To reign with all heaven" is an open channel for expressing the Primal Will-to-Good in Kether. Those who arrive at this stage of development are the incarnate Will of God, the Perfect Law's personal expression. They reign with heaven because all their thoughts, words, and actions are acts of conscious participation in the Divine Life, which flows outward and downward from Kether.

Illuminating Intelligence

The 14th Path is Illuminating Intelligence (Sekhel Meir). It is the essence of electricity (Chashmal). It teaches the fundamentals of the secret mysteries of the Holy Sanctuary and its plan.

ה-נתיב	ארבעה	עשר	נקרא
The Path	4	10	is called

שכל	מאיר	מפני	שהיא
Intelligence	luminous	because	It is
	Illuminating		

עצם	ה-חשמל	ו-ה-מורה	על
essence	shining, amber	& the teacher	of
substance	electricity	instruction	

רזי	יסודות	ה-קדש	ו-תכונתם
mysteries	basics	the sanctuary	& their plan
secret(s)	foundations	holy	
	fundamental	to be consecrated	

The 14th Path is called Illuminating Intelligence because it is "Chasmal," the founder of mysteries and fundament of sanctity and the organization of such matter. It is said to be the path of secrets existing in created beings.

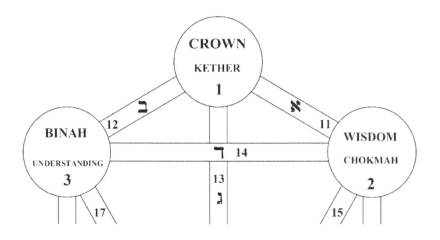

Illuminating Intelligence

This path originates in the Radiant Intelligence of Chokmah, which is the source of its light. Chokmah is like a dynamo, and the Illuminating Intelligence is the light bulb, glowing with incandescence supplied by the current from the power source.

Meir (מאיר) is from the root e'eir (איר), meaning *illustrate*. The three root letters of Meir are e'eir (איר), meaning to *illustrate*. Its spelling resembles Aur (אור), meaning light and fire. Considering the Hebrew letters as pictographs:

Aur (אור) – Light

Letter		Pictograph	Attributions
Aleph	א	Ox head	Root of Air
Vav	ו	Nail	"And"
Resh	ר	head	The Sun, Key 19

Aur, light, is the radiance of the Sun combined with the Element Air. As a symbol, this is shown on the Chariot in Key 7 as the golden disk (Sun) with blue wings (Air).

The letters of e'eir (איר) replace the Vav with Yod, the creative hand. Therefore Meir (מאיר) uses the creative imagination assigned to Key 3 and Daleth (ד) combined with the hand (Yod). This implies light is manipulated and put to use.

Chashmal - חשמל

The text says, "It is the essence of electricity (Chashmal). It teaches the fundamentals of the secret mysteries of the Holy Sanctuary and its plan." In Gesenius' *Hebrew-Chaldee Lexicon to the Old Testament*, p. 313, Chashmal (חשמל) is brass made smooth by polishing. This is the metal of Venus, Daleth (ד) and the Empress. A heart-shaped shield of copper is a prominent feature of the symbolism of Key 3.

Nachash (נחש) designates the metal copper and the serpent in Genesis. Nachash (נחש) is 358, and so is Messiah (משיח), the Redeemer. The Qabalistic mystery concerns the desire nature associated with the Sphere of Venus, Netzach. Desire seems to be the tempter, but we find liberation and redemption by correctly directing the desire force. In Key 3, the copper shield is painted with the Holy Spirit's white dove symbol. When we learn how to manage it, what begins as temptation may be transformed into a shield of protection.

In Appendix 2 of Sefer Yetzirah, Aryeh Kaplan translates chasmal as "speaking silence." Venus rules Taurus, pictured by the Hierophant. This is the teacher *moh.reh* (מורה) in the Hebrew text above. A Latin commentary on the fourteenth path calls Chashmal, *institutrix arcanorum*, "founder of the mysteries." This is also a reference to the Hierophant and Key 5.

Rabbi Ginsburgh adds, "Divinity is perceived first through the חש ('silence') of chashmal (חשמל)." – *The Hebrew Letters*, p. 325.

The Path of Secrets

The text continues, "It is said to be the path of secrets, existing in created beings." Finally, the fourteenth path is the pattern-forming power of creative imagination, which shapes mind-stuff before the externalization of mental patterns into things existing as tangible manifestations.

A careful examination of the symbolism of Key 3 makes one thing clear. Practically every detail of Key 3 is related to reproduction. The central figure is a pregnant woman, the goddess of love and beauty, Aphrodite, or Venus. Roses, her flowers, grow beside her. They are symbols of desire, as well as being the reproductive organs of the plant. Her shield is heart-shaped and is embellished with a dove, a bird sacred to Venus. In Hebrew, the word for dove is *yonah* (יונה). It is from the root yayin (יין), wine. It signifies "to be warm, to ferment, effervescent" (like the seafoam from which Venus is born). Yonah (יונה) is used figuratively for sexual warmth, a characteristic of doves. The waterfall in Key 3 is a vertical column, signifying the male aspect of the life-force (Chaiah, seated in Chokmah), and the pool into which it falls symbolizes the female part of the same force. Finally, the wheat growing at the Empress' feet symbolizes the development and multiplication of seeds.

Fundamentals of the Secret Mysteries

Foundations or fundamentals is *Yesodoth* (יסודות), the plural of Yesod, the name of the ninth Sephirah, attributed to the reproductive activities of both microcosm and macrocosm. Secret mysteries is *rah.zee* (רזי), the plural of *raz* (רז), secret, mysterious, enigmatic. The nature of the secret is revealed in its enumeration, 207. This is the number of *Ain Soph* (אין סוף), no limit and Eternal Lord of the universe (אדון עולם), whose garment is light (אור), which also adds to 207.

The numeration of the words *raziy yesodoth* (רזי יסודות), "secret foundations," is 703. It is the extension of 37 or the sum of the numbers from 0 to 37. Consequently, 703 is a numeral symbol for the complete expression of the power of Yekhidah (יחידה) since Yekhidah is numerically 37.

Furthermore, *ehben* (אבן), stone and *gan* (גן), garden both equal 703 when the final Nun (ן) is reckoned as 700. The symbols of Key 3 emphasize both the garden and the stone bench. Both *ehben* and *gan* are verbal symbols of the Great Work and the controlled and transmuted power in alchemy. This is Yesod's power, reproductive energy shaped by acts of creative imagination.

The fourteenth path deals with the creative, male life-force, identical to the energy steaming through space from the fixed stars or suns as it passes into Binah's field of differentiation and specialization. This activity is the generation, multiplication, and development of the paternal seed (Chaiah in Chokmah) and its mental imagery expression. This activity is both cosmic and personal. The Life-power brings the universe into being through creative imagination. By utilizing the same power, we shape our world and its circumstances in the image of "holiness," which is completeness or perfection.

Our personal life is an elaboration of reproductive function. The chromosomes in the reproductive cells combine to bring forth hereditary tendencies. The gestation process is the outworking of mental patterns in the mother's subconsciousness, modified by the qualities transmitted from the father's ancestral line. However, mental activity is also behind and beneath the physical cell function. This mental activity is subconscious, and during the months of gestation, it epitomizes the entire history of animal evolution. The record of this history is impressed on each human body during pregnancy. Occultists hold that this record's essence is impressed on the Jupiter center cells or solar plexus.

After a child is born, its body grows and changes. This development is a continuation of what was begun at the moment of conception. Subconsciousness is still the dominant factor in body changes from
babyhood to adult life. In childhood, the personal field of human subconsciousness begins to be modified from the self-conscious level.

The earlier influences come from parents, nurses, teachers, or others who have close contact with the child. Later on, as the child's self-consciousness unfolds, his conscious thought and imagination are sources of auto-suggestive influence. Throughout his growth to adulthood, the dominant force in shaping his bodily organism is the power pictured by the Empress – creative imagination.

Even after growth seems to end, mental imagery modifies the body. Our secret thoughts and feelings are written on our faces. For those who know how to read the record, they are inscribed in our hands.

What is not so well understood is that the power of creative imagination can be used consciously to make changes in the physical vehicle. It is possible to effect internal changes in the body, which take one out of ordinary humanity's limitations into the Fifth Kingdom. Creative imagination is how the life-force in Chokmah affects subtle physiological changes that raise one to the Grade of Master of the Temple, attributed to Binah, where the fourteenth path completes itself.

Eliphas Levi's manuscript says adept masters of Daleth's path enable them to influence others. Spiritual healers begin by perfecting their physical organisms. Thus they become open channels for a current of the cosmic life-force. The mind directs the healing method, but it is not an ordinary psychotherapeutic procedure. The highest spiritual healing is not a simple suggestion or physical magnetism. It directly applies the cosmic life-force, controlled by mental imagery.

Healers who employ this type of spiritual therapy have a sensation when so doing. They feel the life-force flowing out of them into the patient's body, as did Jesus when the woman touched the hem of his garment.

Yet even they must have suitable mental preparation in the persons they heal. Faith on the part of the patient is indispensable for a permanent cure. Jesus said, "Your faith has made you whole." Yet, it is a mistake to suppose that faith is the only healing agency. Faith makes the patient receptive. However, a higher spiritual healing flows a current of life-force through the healer's organism.

Such a healer has completed what alchemists call the "confection of the Philosophers' Stone." So it is the Stone and the Garden concerning which we have written.

Besides *eben* (אבן) being the combination of *Ab* (אב) with *Ben* (בן), Father with Son, eben is a symbol of the power designated by Ab. Ab is the life-force in Chokmah, as expressed through Nun (נ). The energy operates primarily through the reproductive system governed by Scorpio (♏).

Ojas - The illuminating

The Sanskrit Ojas, "the illuminating or bright," stands for the sublimated sexual energy and is the seat of the life-force in Chokmah, the Illuminating Intelligence. Concerning Ojas, Swami Vivekananda writes:

"The lowest center is where all energy becomes stored up, which has to be taken from there and brought to the last one, the brain. The Yogis claim that of all the energies, the human body comprises the highest in what they call 'Ojas.' Now, this Ojas is stored up in the brain, and the more the Ojas is in a man's head, the more powerful he is, the more intellectual and the more spiritually strong a human will be. This is the action of Ojas. One man may speak beautiful language and thoughts, but they do not impress people; another man speaks neither beautiful language nor beautiful thoughts, yet his words charm. That is the power of Ojas coming out. Therefore, every movement coming from him will be powerful.

"Now, in all humanity, there is more or less of this Ojas stored up. All the forces working in the body, in their highest form, become Ojas. Remember that it is only a question of transformation. The same force which is working outside, as electricity or magnetism, will become changed into Ojas. The Yogis say that that part of the human energy, expressed as sex energy, sexual functions, sexual thought, and so on, easily becomes Ojas when checked and controlled. As this lowest center is the one that guides all these functions, therefore the Yogi pays particular attention to that center. He tries to take up all this sexual energy and convert it into Ojas. It is only the chaste man or woman who can make Ojas rise and become stored in the brain, and that is why chastity has always been considered the highest virtue, because man feels that if he is unchaste, spirituality goes away, he loses mental vigor, and strong moral stamina. That is why in all religious orders that have produced spiritual giants, you will always find this intense chastity insisted upon." – Raja Yoga, pp. 59-61.

This quote identifies the force inside the body with electricity and magnetism. It is radiant energy at work in the Sphere of the Zodiac (Chokmah). Ojas is a transformation of the forces which work as muscular strength. In Western occultism, muscle tone is under the rulership of Mars, which also rules the sexual energy, which is changed into Ojas.

We feel it necessary to say that we would substitute Vivekananda's words, controlled and checked for the more accurate terms, "sublimated and redirected." Swami Vivekananda is correct on the ascetic disciplines as bringing about an intensification of the Ojas. For some forms of training, complete abstinence from sex relations is necessary. However, there is a difference between abstinence and continence. Jeremy Taylor points out: "Chastity is either abstinence or continence: abstinence is that of virgins or widows: continence, that of married persons."

Continence is by no means incompatible with everyday living. Overindulgence wastes power. Chastity is concerned with physical and mental activity. A mind preoccupied with sexual imagery wastes as much energy as an unrestrained body. One of the weaknesses of our modern life is over-indulgence in erotic imagery. Popular fiction, movies, and the stage all contribute to this over-stimulus. Until it is corrected, we may expect both sexes' minds and bodies, particularly adolescents and young adults, to be seriously harmed by this unwholesome emphasis on sex.

The remedy is not a puritanical insistence on abstinence. The difficulty is found in widespread errors concerning sex that it's sinful and impure. The power whereby the One Ego provides itself with physical bodies is inherently pure. It is truly sacred, and recognizing this is of paramount importance to receive the benefits resulting from its direction and sublimation.

CHAPTER 9

15th Path of Heh - ה

Stable Intelligence

The 15th Path is Stable Intelligence (Sekhel Ma'amid). From the pure darkness, it stabilizes the essence of Creation (Briah). But, the Masters say, "wrapped it in thick darkness." – Job 38:9.

ה-נתיב	החמשה	עשר	נקרא
The Path	5	10	is called

שכל	מעמיד	ו-נקרא	כן
Consciousness	stable	is called	Yes, truly

מפני	שהוא	מעמיד	עצם
because	It is	stability	essence
			substance

ה-בריאה	כ-ערפלי	טהור	ו-בעלי
Briah, creation	darkness	pure	masters

העיון	אמרו	כי	הוא
Theory	they said	because	Hu
			It, he

ה-ערפל	ו-זהו	ו-ערפל	ה-תולתו
darkness	and - that is	fog	curly
gloom	this is		band
wrapped it in thick darkness			

The 15th Path is called the Constituting Intelligence because it constitutes the creation "in the darkness of the world." The philosophers said it is the darkness that Job talks about in the Scripture: "and the dark cloud its wrapping." Therefore, it is also called the path of the aperture of light.

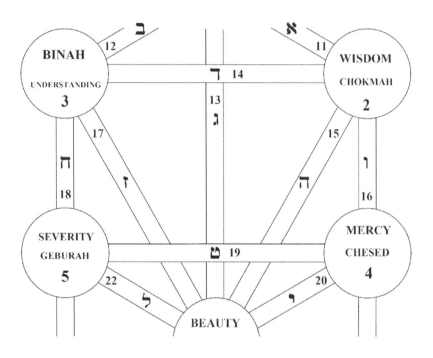

The fifteenth path is Heh (ה), symbolized by the Emperor. It carries the power of Wisdom, the second Sephirah, to Beauty, the sixth. It is the link between the life-force Chaiah (חיה), identical to the radiant energy of fixed stars, suns, and the One Ego. The central One Self radiant energy is distributed to all human personalities, incarnate and discarnate. Each person is like a radio receiving set. The One Ego is the CENTRAL INTELLIGENCE or broadcasting center for the human race. From Chokmah, Chaiah, the life-force is sent forth to the One Ego and is distributed to every human being.

The universal creative force (Chaiah) is identical to living organisms' procreative power. The *Bhagavad-Gita* says: "My great Prakriti is the womb into which I cast the seed. From this is the birth of all creatures."

Chokmah, the source of the fifteenth path, is called Ab, the Father. In every one of the three paths proceeding from this second Sephirah, the essential potency is masculine.

Letter Heh ה

The Menachot (meal offering) has this to say about the letter Heh:

"Isaiah (26:4) is usually translated: 'Trust in G-d forever, for in Y-ah, [who is] G-d, is the everlasting rock.' However, the prefix translated here as "in" can also mean "through" or "by,"; and the divine name Y-ah is spelled *yud-hei* (יה), the word for "rock" (tzur, צור) can also be taken as a verb meaning "to form," and the word for "everlasting" ("olamim") can also mean "worlds." Thus, the verse can be mystically translated as: "Trust in G-d forever, for with the letters Yud and Heh G-d formed the worlds." Based on this (and other verses), the Sages say that G-d created This World with the letter Heh and the World to Come with the letter Yud." – Menachot 29b

"The ordinal beginning of the alef-beit is the letter alef. Phonetically, the vapor, amorphic 'matter' from which the pronunciation of every letter is formed, is the secret of the letter heh." – The Hebrew Letters, p. 296.

146

The letter name, Heh (הה), value is 10, the same as Yod ('),
symbolized by the Hermit. The first Heh of הה represents *insight*
or the Life-power's knowledge of itself. The second Heh is a
symbol of *foresight*, directed toward the outcome following from
what *insight* reveals. The Emperor faces north, which refers to the
future on the Tree of Life (left-hand pillar). It is the side of the
unknown and the unmanifest. From the left side come our
problems. The Northside is the hidden forces that arouse our fears.
To the left side, we mentally formulate plans leading to more
perfected manifestation.

Stable Intelligence

Ma'amid (מעמיד) means, meaning "to rise, to stand erect." This
stability comes from the thick darkness where God dwells. This is
our source of stability and the essence of creation.

The phallic significance of, *standing erect,* is confirmed by the
attribution of the sign Aries. Mars rules Aries. The dominant
power in the 15th Path is the Mars-force, the active generative
principle in nature. The universal creative force, *Chaiah*, is
identical to living organisms' procreative power.

The "creative force" is *etzem ha-briah* (עצם ה-בריאה), literally "essence of creation." Etzem is related to radiant energy because its value is 200. This is the number of Resh (ר) and the Sun. The second word is spelled with the prefixed Heh (ה-בריאה) and adds to 223.

223 is the value of the mysterious word Abrech (אברך), which means "tender father." *The Fama Fraternitatis* calls the Founder of the Order "Father R. C.," which, written in Hebrew, would be Ab (אב) Roke (רך) or, Abrech.

Hence, *etzem ha-briah* (עצם ה-בריאה) signifies the essential nature of the paternal force, which is concentrated in Kether, and then becomes the radiant life-force in the second Sephirah.

Another arrangement of the same letters for ha-Briah (ה-בריאה) may be read as היה ברא, hahyah (היה), "to be," and beraw (ברא), "to create." The inner meaning is the essential characteristic of *being* is, *creativity*. Creation is not an event that took place long ago. The Life-power is eternally creative, as we affirm in *The Pattern on the Trestleboard*.

From pure darkness, it stabilizes the essence of Creation. The creative force is stabilized or "made to rise" in pure darkness. *Tahoor* (טהור) means pure and is connected with Yesod. This suggests that creativity is sexual energy. Yesod is the archetypal Adam's generative forces seat, the One Ego seated in Tiphareth. Furthermore, the name of the ninth Sephirah, *Yesod* (יסוד), can be written *Sod Yod* (י סוד), "Secret of Yod." The "secret" has a double meaning because Yod (י) symbolizes the phallus.

Pure darkness is the creative force. The obscurity of the universal subconscious plane is represented by the ninth path of Yesod. Subconsciousness is the basis or foundation of all manifestations. It is the plane where the Constituting Intelligence sets the creative force in motion. The Physical plane (Malkuth) is the "great womb" into which the seed of creation is cast. Hence, in Key 4's background, on a level below where the Emperor sits, flows a river that symbolizes the stream of subconscious activity— the stream of the cosmic creative force, or Water of Life.

Darkness is, o'ra.pel (ערפל). The sequence of letters is represented by Keys 15, 19, 16, and 11. The uninitiated regard darkness as terror, mystery, and evil. It is the devil of exoteric dogmatism.

On the other hand, initiates perceive a radiant darkness, behind which is the liberating, regenerative power typified by Key 19. The creative force is symbolized as the flash of lightning in Key 16, tearing down the prison of false science. This radiant darkness is the source of the power of adjustment, which preserves the balance of forces in action throughout the universe, symbolized by Key 11.

Key 4, the Emperor

The initiate possessing the powers of the path "can neither be surprised by misfortune, nor overwhelmed by disasters, nor conquered by his enemies." The first two powers indicate the quality of foresight, a characteristic of Aries. The third is a manifestation of the Martian fighting quality.

The Emperor symbolizes these traits. He is armed, so that nothing can harm him. His crown, globe and scepter are symbols of dominion. The occult meaning of Key 4 includes the powers of insight and foresight indicated by the attribute of vision assigned to Heh (ה).

Ageless Wisdom says the creative act is a projection of the Life-power's clear vision of its nature into the field of subconsciousness. Thus Hindu books tell us Purusha is the *Onlooker* and that Prakriti, the power of nature, works because Purusha looks on.

The force of the Emperor is your force. Yours is the power that cannot be surprised by misfortune, overwhelmed by disasters, or overcome by enemies. Yours is the original creative power. At this instant, it constitutes creation in the pure darkness of your subconsciousness.

It operates principally through the organs of sight. All personal experience of vision is an expression of the cosmic Power-to-See. To the degree that you see things as they are, your personality is a channel for the original creative power.

The picture of the Emperor will help you perfect the organs of vision. It sets a perfect pattern for subconsciousness to work out in body structure. When you look at it, say to yourself, "This is my I

AM, as it really is." The fifteenth path is rooted in the unfailing Wisdom of the One Life. Bear in mind that it completes itself in Beauty.

Your vision will change as your body changes subtly under the influence of this pictured suggestion. More and more will the True World's radiant beauty (veiled by our ignorance) become evident. More will become more aware of the working of the creative force within your being. More and more, your daily experience demonstrates to you that creation is eternal. Something with an irresistible tendency toward producing beautiful results flows through your thoughts, words, and actions.

Eternal Intelligence

The 16th Path is Eternal Intelligence (Sekhel Nitz.chi). It is the pleasure (Eden) of Glory. There is no Glory beneath it (like it). It is called the Garden of Eden, prepared for the Merciful Ones (Saints).

נקרא	עשר	ששה	ה-נתיב
is called	10	6	The Path

כן	ו-נקרא	נצחי	שכל
truly	is called	eternal infinite	Intelligence

ה-כבוד	עדון	שהוא	מפני
The glory	Eden, garden pleasure	It is	because

ל-מטה	כבוד	שאין
like it beneath	glory	There is no

שם	שהוא	כמו	הימנה
Shem – name	It is	same as	There

עדן	גן	הנקרא	והוא
Eden	garden	called	Hu, and it

חסד	ל-**חסדים**	חמוכן
Chesed- Mercy	reward of the	prepared

152

The 16th Path is called the Triumphant and Eternal Intelligence since it is the very joy of glory, which is similar to it, and it is called the Paradise of delight, which has been prepared for honest people. It is also the path of victory against evil geniuses.

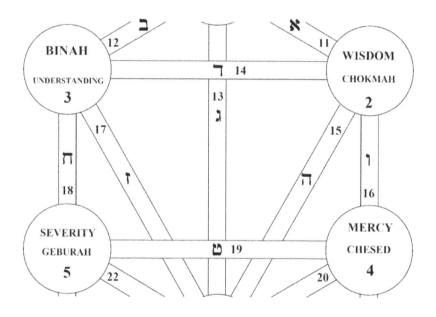

Eternal Consciousness

Nitz.chi (נצחי) means eternal, perpetual, everlasting, agelong, and infinite. This adjective is derived from the noun Netzach (נצח) Victory, the seventh Sephirah. In dealing with our problems, to those who open their interior hearing, the Voice of the Master speaks.

"In the beginning of Creation, when Infinite Light filled all of reality, G-d contracted his Light to create hollow empty space, as it were, the "place" necessary for the existence of finite worlds. Into this vacuum, G-d drew down a single line of light, figuratively speaking, from the Infinite Source. This ray of light is the secret of the letter Vav. Though the line is singular in appearance, it nonetheless possesses two dimensions, an external and an internal force, both of which take part in the process of Creation and the continuous interaction between the creative power and the created reality." *The Hebrew Letters*, p. 94

Letter Name Vav

The letter-name Vav (וו) is 12. This is the number of the Divine Name Hu (הוא), the third personal pronoun corresponding to "He." This is a Divine Name associated with the first Sephirah, Kether. Therefore, the Hierophant symbolizes the Cosmic One Self, Yekhidah, acting as the Inner Teacher of humanity.

Taurus ♉

The fifteenth path is represented by the Hierophant associated with Taurus, ruled by Venus. Venus corresponds to the fourteenth path of Daleth (ד) and creative imagination. All cosmic or personal imagination is the elaboration and development of ideas preserved by memory.

The Moon (High Priestess) is exalted in Taurus. The High Priestess symbolizes subconsciousness as the recorder of experience, and her scroll typifies memory. It is the Book of Cosmic experience.

Personal memory is connected to the Universal Being (the nail, Vav) because our memory is a chapter and an integral part of the cosmic record. By properly using our recollection power, we consciously unite our memory with the Life-power. While we are caught in the net of the dream of separateness, we do not share the cosmic recollection. When we learn to listen, we hear the Voice, teaching us from within. When we become aware of this Voice, we understand that it has been speaking for all eternity in the temple's inner shrine of human personality. We do not always hear, but the Voice still speaks and has influenced our lives. Our subconscious systems of knowledge and desire (the two ministers kneeling before the Hierophant) are modified when it speaks. In due course, these personal ministers of the One Self prepare us to enter the Inner Shrine.

The sixteenth path is called "the delight [pleasure] of glory" because we are filled with joy when we receive the instruction. Hence every communication we receive from the Inner Voice reveals the same truth concerning the ONE POWER, which Hindus call "Existence-Knowledge-Bliss Absolute."

The sixteenth path is called the Garden of Eden (עדן גן) or "delight." The garden holds the lilies and roses at the Magician's feet. It is also the garden wherein the Empress sits. *Gan* (גן) and *ehben* (אבן) (stone) are numerically 53 and stand for the state of conscious identification of the One Ego with the cosmic or universal One Self. They represent the state of consciousness from which humanity was driven in Genesis's allegory of the fall.

This state may be regained. It is "prepared for the compassionate." These are the Chasidim (חסדים), who are filled with the spirit of the fourth Sephirah. They are members of the grade called "Exempt Adept" or "Masters of Compassion." They are men and women receptive to the influx of the lifeforce, which flows through the sixteenth path from Chokmah to Chesed. They know how to open themselves to the influx, which flows down into human personality from superconscious levels. They may be identified by one salient characteristic. They are unfailingly merciful.

Levi's old manuscript assigns Vav's power: "He knows the reason of the past, present, and future." This is the constant state of mind of an Exempt Adept or Master of Compassion. The reason, or cause, of time, is eternity. When it considers the eternal NOW, past, present, and future are the divisions made by the intellect. This NOW is known in the manifestation of the Eternal Intelligence through a human mind.

Therefore, The Hierophant sits in the center and faces us. Like the High Priestess, he is between two pillars. He is the same as the angel in Key 14 because 14 reduces to 5 and indicates his identity. He is the World Dancer in Key 21, representing the full manifestation of his eternal self-revelation. Note that 5 extends to 6 (the sum of the numbers from 0 to 5 is 15). Reduced to one digit, 15 is 6. Twenty-one (21) is the extension of 6 ($1+2+3+4+5+6 = 21$). Therefore, the number 21, the last key of the Tarot, represents the Hierophant's power's fullest expression.

An Exempt Adept, or Master of Compassion, enjoys continual communication with what we picture as the Hierophant. That is why they are "Exempt." They are released from the delusion of separateness. They are a conduit for Chesed's benevolence, and it manifests through them as a tireless activity. They are free from effort and struggle. For them, the Eternal Being is a direct perception. "Before Abraham was, I AM." The Eternal Being is the cause of the past, present, and future.

How may this union be affected? First, it concerns the functions of three centers in the human body.

1. These are the auditory center in the brain,
2. the Moon center (pituitary gland),
3. the Venus center in the throat.

In their combined activity, one hears the "still, small voice," the same that spoke to Jesus, "As I hear, I judge, and my judgment is just." The functioning of these three centers is brought about by a fourfold method.

1. The adoption of the receptive, listening, devotional attitude is shown by the two figures kneeling before the Hierophant. That is to say, by devotion to the One Life above and within the human personality and by recognizing that Life is a limitless source of wisdom, the Father of all that exists.

2. Continually exercising memory in recalling that ALL POWER is present everywhere. By reminding ourselves time and time again that our senses report nothing whatsoever to us other than the Eternal Presence of the Divine Glory – kabode (כבוד).

3. Using imagination in every way ingenuity can suggest discriminating between the One Thing's gross appearances and the subtle Reality that these appearances veil. Using imagination to make vivid your awareness of the meaning of the Eternal Presence in even the slightest detail of whatever you perceive.

4. The practice of genuine compassion or mercy. This fourth rule is the most important of all. The "Garden of Eden" is prepared for the benevolent. "Benevolence," which means "goodwill," must be expressed in thought, word, and deed.

We must live to bless all humanity, all creatures, and all conditions. The last is the hardest. Every situation is subject to improvement. Condemnation arrests improvement while blessing furthers it. Benevolence must be given in words of praise, helpfulness, and the kind of action that backs up the words with deeds of loving service. To bless is always to be blessed. To give freely is the sure way to receive abundantly.

OBTW.

Admonishing someone for their ignorant or evil deeds is not condemnation. Also, benevolence is not unconditional forgiveness. If someone continues to abuse you, walk away. Let the dead bury the dead.

Back to the text.

Union with superconsciousness is the object of every religion. True religion is the tie that binds personal consciousness to the ALL. The symbols of Key 5 suggest the Hierophant is teaching religion.

Goodwill is the Magical Will

The kind of thinking, saying, and doing we have outlined brings about subtle personality changes, which are the preliminaries to union or yoga. Benevolence has a specific physiological effect. Practicing kindness is the only way to effect this change. Goodwill to humanity, to all creatures, to all conditions, is an active force. Goodwill, even during this world crisis, as shown in Key 16, is a catastrophe that clears the way for a better understanding and practical expression of humanity's unity.

Goodwill is the only valid magical will. It purifies the personal consciousness and nerve currents, cleanses the bloodstream, and purifies the whole body. It affects the glandular secretions and liberates into the blood the chemical elements with which the body must be supplied before there are results.

Try it, and see for yourself.

CHAPTER 10

17th Path of Zain - ז

Perceptive Intelligence

The 17th Path is Perceptive Intelligence (Sekhel Ha.her.gesh). It is prepared for the Faithful Ones (Saints) so they are clothed with the Holy Spirit. It is called the Foundation (Yesod) of Beauty (Tiphareth) and is placed among the Supernals (upper realms).

ה-נתיב	שבעה	עשר	נקרא
The Path	7	10	is called

שכל	ה-הרגש	ו-הוא	מוכן
Intelligence	the senses	and it	prepared
	excite	Hu	ready
	perceptive		

ל-חסידי	ה-אמונה	ל-ה-תלבשא	בו
Merciful Ones	faith, belief	to dress	with
Saints		clothed	

ב-רוח	קדושה	ו-הוא	נקרא
Rauch	holy	and it	is called
soul, spirit		Hu	

יסוד	ה-תפארת	ב-מעמד	ה-עליונים
Yesod	Tiphareth	at the place	The upper(s)
foundation	the beauty		Height
basis			Supernal

The 17th Path is called the Disposing Intelligence, which prepares the Christian faith for the devout so that, through it, they shall be covered by the Holy Spirit, and it is said to be the fundament of beauty by the condition of Supreme entities. Moreover, it supervises all superior and inferior forms.

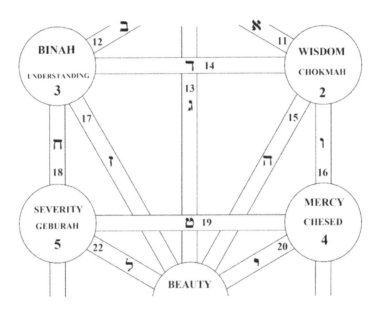

The seventeenth path is Zain (ז), symbolized by the Lovers. It is the first path projected from Binah and joins Tiphareth. Thus it is the link connecting the Divine Soul with the EGO. The Path of Zain suggests the operation of the Supernal Understanding *in separating the creatures produced* by the Constituting Intelligence into species, classes, etc. The fundamental separation is sex; hence, this path is Zain, the Sword and the Lovers.

Letter Name Zain זִין

Zain (זִין) means a weapon and especially a sword. "The sword, the prototype weapon of war, symbolizes the conflict inherent in physical reality. Though it does not initially seem so, conflict – like all-natural phenomena – is purposeful and constructive. Through the seeming external necessity to confront one's enemy in battle, and often to even physically wrestle him (as did Jacob with the archangel of Esau), previously opposite attributes subconsciously merge, elevating one to a higher state of existence." *The Hebrew Letters*, p. 113.

Perceptive Intelligence

Hergesh (הרגש) means *feeling, sensation,* and *emotion.* It is similar to the spelling of Murgash (מורגש) in the twenty-seventh path of Peh. Murgash means *felt, perceptible,* and *noticeable.*

The Master of Reception chooses their words carefully. It suggests that the 17th Path of Perceptive or Feeling Intelligence is linked to the 27th Path of Perceptible or Felt Intelligence. And so the sword (Zain) is linked with Mars (Peh), the warrior.

163

Key 6 includes symbols connected with the idea of intense, flaming activity. Closer inspection will correct the impression of placidity created by the surface appearance of the design. First of all, the hair of the angel is flaming. Behind the man is a tree bearing twelve fiery fruits. Behind the woman is a tree with five fruits, referring to the senses. Around the trunk of the tree is coiled a serpent.

Thus the symbolism is related to the title of the seventeenth path. The title of Key 6, The Lovers, implies the forces represented are far from being cool and calm. Love is warm, and the violence of lovers is proverbial.

Qabalistic analysis of the word *ha-hergesh* adds much to our knowledge of the seventeenth path's occult meaning. Let us consider this word, letter by letter,

First *Heh* (ה) – Hebrew article corresponding to English "the." It calls for specific attention. A house can be any house. However, "the house" means a particular home. Binah is assigned to the letter Heh. Binah is that which particularizes and sets up distinctions, limitations, and boundaries.

Second *Heh* - Aries, a cardinal fire sign.

Resh (ר), to which the Sun is attributed. It corresponds to Key 19, which is a Tarot symbol of regeneration.

Gimel (ג) is the letter of the Moon. This is the Tarot High Priestess and the thirteenth path of wisdom.

Shin (ש), which is attributed to the element of fire. Shin also stands for Ruach Elohim, the Spirit of God.

Ha-hergesh (הה-הרגש) can be read as "The (ה) Sun (ר), Moon (ג), and fire (ש). Or using the alchemical attributions, "The (Heh) Gold (Resh), Silver (Gimel) and the Quintessence (Shin)." The spiritual fire is the alchemist's quintessence and is often symbolized by a circle divided into eight equal segments. It is shown on the Wheel of Fortune's center and the wheels on Fool's robe. Hence one of the ornaments is marked with the letter Shin (ש).

165

The Sun and Moon perform the Great Work with Mercury's aid in alchemical books. The symbolism of Key 6 illustrates this. The man corresponds to the alchemical sun, and behind him is a tree with twelve fruits, representing the sun's twelve signs or mansions. The woman corresponds to the alchemical moon. The mountain in the background is a symbol of the work. The angel is Raphael, the angel of Mercury.

The Yogis, in their books, mention two aspects of the Life-Breath – Prana. The positive, male part is Surya, the sun. The negative female aspect is Rayi, the moon. Surya is the hot, driving, violent current of Prana. Rayi is the cool, responsive lunar current, and impressibility distinguishes it.

The solar and lunar currents work through the human body's two halves, chiefly along the sympathetic system's nerves—the solar current works through the right half, called Pingala. The lunar current works through the left half named Ida. These names apply to the left-hand and right-hand divisions of the nerves composing the sympathetic system.

The alternation of these two currents of energy is what the alchemist utilizes, what the Yogi employs in developing inner powers, and what the magicians adapt to their purposes. The key to all occult ability is the right discrimination between the natures of these two currents of force, and correct discrimination is the Magician's sword or Zain (זין).

The use of the sword is the "narrow way of attainment." Hence Jesus said he would bring a sword. Mohammed said the way to Paradise is over a bridge narrow as a razor's edge. The Emerald

Tablet says, "Separate the earth from the fire, the subtle from the gross, suavely, and with great ingenuity."

A Hindu book declares: "To those men who practice and keep the sun and moon in proper order, knowledge of the past and future becomes as easy as if they were in their hand." And again: "The moon is checked by the sun, and the sun by the moon; he who knows this practice strides in a moment over the three worlds."

In this context, the three worlds are past, present, and future. A practical occultist, whether called a Yogi, magician, or alchemist, can cut the Gordian Knot of time with the sword of discrimination.

When the solar and lunar currents of the Life-power are rightly perceived and discriminated, when their operation is kept in proper order, the personality of the individual engaged in this practice becomes a free, unobstructed channel for the outpouring of the cosmic life-force. Thus our text says Perceptive Intelligence clothes the compassionate with the Holy Life-Breath.

The compassionate are the Chasidim or Masters of Compassion. They are clothed or invested with all the powers of the Spirit. Their consciousness is pictured by Key 6.

In ordinary speech, breath is air. To be "clothed with breath" is shown in Key 6. The two human figures represent self-consciousness and subconsciousness and are nude to show that the right discrimination strips these two modes of personal consciousness of all disguises. A Master of Compassion has brought this to pass. They are free from guile and concealment. They established a balance between the "sun" and the "moon" between the self-conscious and subconscious personality modes. Solar current is connected with the functions of self-conscious life

167

for the hot, electric. The cool, magnetic lunar flow is at work through subconsciousness.

Knowledge of the order of the solar and lunar currents and the power to control them is not gained from books or lessons. The aspirant is told: "You must learn this from the Guru," never: "You must learn this from a Guru." This means that there is one Guru, one Teacher. It is pictured as the Hierophant. From this one Teacher, all higher wisdom and mastery secrets are received. The One Teacher makes them known to those ready, and He knows when they are ready. His pupils receive instruction through the operation of Neshamah, the Divine Soul seated in Binah.

Books and lessons are useful. They put us on the track of the path which leads to the Guru. They show the preliminary practices. They lay down rules of thought, speech, and conduct, which enable us to become sufficiently receptive to merit the name "Qabalist." Our part is to travel the path and put the rules into action. An irrevocable law of nature bars us from the presence of the One Teacher if we do not practice. The Guru never accepts lazy pupils. He speaks eternally to all humanity. However, his instruction falls unheeded on deaf ears. Ability to hear his voice is the fruit of practice.

Nature is our first teacher. She sets the solar and lunar currents coursing through our bodies long before we wake from our nightmare of separateness. Our Mother prepares us. She is like a woman who hears her child crying at night and finds the little one struggling in the throes of a bad dream. Gently she wakes, comforts, and shows us there is nothing to fear. Years before anyone knows they are interested in the higher knowledge, the Great Mother – the Divine Soul –is gently nudging them to wake from their tortured dream. While they still sleep, her endeavors to

168

arouse them are incorporated into their nightmare. Yet it is only the Mother, full of compassion, bringing them to realization.

While remaining in the dream's grip, her touch frightens the dreamers more. They believe it to be a tiger of disease, a wolf of poverty, a lion of oppression, and a serpent of sin. The experiences designed to liberate them are interpreted as all dangers and miseries. When the dream ends, they know that the Mother was only shaking them into wakefulness so they might be released from their pain and terror.

When we wake, she takes us by the hand and guides us in her ways. This contact with reality is said in our text to "establish the faith of the compassionate." Theirs is faith expressed by action, as shown in Key 11. It means Amen (אמן) or "So be it" to all experiences because it understands every event's meaning.

Foundation of Beauty

Hence the Disposing Intelligence is called the "Foundation of Tiphareth in the plane of the Supernals." The power active in this path is the Divine Soul, symbolized in Key 6 by the angel Raphael. The plane of the Supernals is the three upper Sephiroth: Kether (Will), Chokmah (Wisdom), and Binah (Understanding). Binah is the Yesod, or Foundation, of Tiphareth, because without Understanding the One Ego, Tiphareth would have no firm basis.

Neither Will nor Wisdom are enough to provide that basis. Understanding is Love, and without the firm foundation of Love, there would be no stability in the One Ego. It is not enough to will. It is not enough to be wise. Love is what makes purpose and grasp of principles effectively.

169

Grade of Master of the Temple

In the Grades of the True and Invisible Rosicrucian Order, the Master of the Temple is assigned to Binah. They who attain it are filled with the power of the Divine Soul. This power is the angel in Key 6. The power flows down from Kether to Binah through the twelfth path channel, symbolized by Key 1. It is the alchemical Mercury, which directs the Sun and Moon. This same Mercury is the ruling principle of Zain's path, which is also Gemini's.

Discrimination is the fruit of love. Love conquers death. Love confers the gift of immortality. Love opens the door to the fourth dimension. As St. Paul wrote:

"I kneel before the Father from whom every family in heaven or on earth takes its name and beg him out of his wealth of glory to strengthen you mightily through his Spirit in your inner nature and through your faith to let Christ in his love, make his home in your hearts. Your roots must be deep and your foundations strong so that you and all God's people may be strong enough to grasp what breadth, length, height, and depth mean, and to understand Christ's love, so far beyond our understanding so that you may be filled with the very fulness of God." – Ephesians 3:14 - 21

This is one of the most profound passages in the New Testament. The "glory" of which it speaks is that same radiant energy. The Christ is the One Ego of all humanity, one with Ab, the paternal life-force in Chokmah. The great secret is the "mystery of Christ." That mystery is a secret concerning space, and Paul hints at this by speaking of breadth, length, and height – the three dimensions – and adding depth (Βαθος), a noun used symbolically throughout the New Testament to designate the Fourth Dimension, the Great Within.

Masters of the Temple filled with an understanding of the perfect law, are continually guided by the Divine Soul. They rule their bodies and their circumstances in ways that seem miraculous. They exercise the powers in Levi's manuscript in connection with the path of Zain. They "possess the secret of the resurrection of the dead and the key of immortality." They triumph over death because their consciousness is one with that of the Ever-living. In the Tarot Tableau, Key 6 is the top picture in a vertical row of three. Beneath it is Key 13, Death. Below Key 13 is Key 20, a symbol of the resurrection.

Intelligence of the House of Influx

The 18th Path is called the Intelligence of the House of Influx (Sekhel Bet ha.she.fah). From investigations, a secret is transmitted (attracted) to all who dwell (cleave) in its shadow. Those who walk the 18th Path bind themselves to investigate the substance (reality) transmitted (emanating) from the Cause of Causes.

שכל	נקרא	שמונה	ה-נתיב
Intelligence	is called	8	The Path

חקירותו	ו-מתוך	ה-שפע	בית
probe, investigate	from, of, out of	Influence influx abundance	house

יתלוננים	העבר	רז	מושכים
he-will-rest Ps. 90:1	transmit	secret mystery	attracting

ממשותו	ב-חקירות	ו-הדבקים	ב-עלו
reality, effect Substance, materialize	probe investigate	& cleave bind	in its (shadow)

		העילות	מעילת
		of causes	cause

The 18th Path is called the Intelligence of the House of Influence because by the middle of its meticulous research, mysteries are drawn, as long as the obscure meanings which are hidden in its shadows, and the things, which are interlinked to its ipseity (individual identity, selfhood), are drawn from the Cause of the Causes. (This sentence doesn't make sense to me; however, that's the Latin text.)

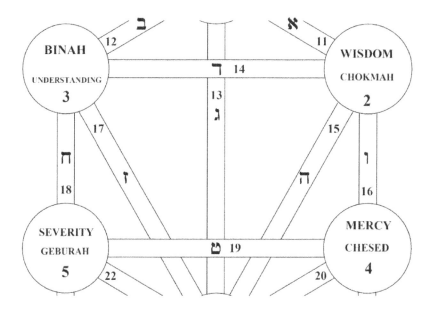

The eighteenth path of wisdom is Cheth (ח). It is the second path from Binah, carrying down the influence that energizes Geburah.

Letter Chet ח

"The form of the letter *chet* resembles a gateway. Through a gateway, one enters and exits. One enters an inner realm or chamber with a deeper awareness and a truer experience level. One exit to return to one's previous, stable state of existence, infused with the light of one's new experience." – *The Hebrew Letters*, p. 125.

Influence - Shefah

Shefah (שפע), meaning influence, suggests water. The Hebrew shefah occurred once in the Old Testament (Deuteronomy 33:19) and was translated as *abundance*. "They shall suck the abundance of the seas." Here the idea of abundance is directly connected with water. In this passage, there is also an occult reference to time because the word for "seas," *yomim* (ימים), is identical to the spelling "days."

The power is like water because Cheth corresponds to Cancer, a cardinal water sign. The power comes in waves. It runs in currents. It ebbs and flows. It is purifying, and in it, all forms are held, either in suspension or solution. Often it is compared to a vast ocean. Thus Binah, the eighteenth path source, is called the Great Sea and the Great Mother.

In Key 7, a river flows behind the chariot to represent the eternal flow of conscious energy. That stream of power coming beyond the limits of personality is the cause of all activity within those limits.

Key 7 – The Chariot

In Key 7, the background houses refer to Beth's Path, which joins Kether to Binah. The walled city refers to Binah, for the "Holy City" symbolizes Binah and the Sanctifying Intelligence. With other design details, the chariot and the charioteer give a martial aspect to this Tarot Key. The picture's background relates to the Sephirah from which the Path of Cheth begins, Binah. The foreground refers to the Sphere of Mars, the seat of Volition, in which the Path of Cheth is completed.

Analysis of Shefah

Tarot symbols aid us in grasping the inner significance of shefah (שׁפע). Its first letter (שׁ) is represented by Key 20, a symbol of the Fourth Dimension, the plane of being above and within all other planes. Key 20 shows the coffins of personal consciousness floating on the Great Sea, Binah, the boundless ocean of Divine Understanding. The second letter, Peh (פ), corresponds to Key 16. It shows another aspect of the power as the lightning-flash, which destroys the tower of false science. This flash symbolizes Mezla, the Holy Influence, which descends from Kether to establish the ten Sephiroth. The last letter, Ayin (ע), corresponds to Key 15. It shows how our sensation reports interpret the same power from superficial appearances. Then it poses riddles to us. Hence the sphinxes which draw the chariot are related to the Devil. Like him, they are bizarre combinations of human and animal forms.

The sphinxes and the Devil are types of the Great Magical Agent, the hidden force employed in practical occultism. The sphinxes also symbolize the Great Arcanum, whereby the power is controlled. They combine the lion and the woman, signifying Key 8, where the woman controls the lion and is joined to him by a chain of roses.

Numerically, shefah (שׁפע) is 450. This is 10 x 45, or Adam (אדם), 45, multiplied by the ten Sephiroth. 450 is also the number of *lookhuth* (לוחות), the tables on which Moses wrote the law. Here is a suggestion that all the powers of man are developments of the Tora. TORA is inscribed on the scroll of the High Priestess, who corresponds to the Moon, ruler of Cancer. Since the manifestation of the Tora is the result of the reactions among the ten sephiroth, 450 is also the number of peree etz (פרי עץ), the Fruit of the Tree.

In the evolution of these powers through humanity and beyond, "sin" appears. The same letters rearranged spell *pahshah* (פשע), meaning *crime* or *misdeed*. Here Peh is put before the Shin instead of after it. That is to say, the tower of personality is placed before the liberty of spiritual realization symbolized by Key 20.

Volition

The path of Cheth ends in Geburah, the seat of volition, or "personal will." Geburah has three names, Fear, Severity, and Justice. Qabalists identify volition with the impersonal law, which terrifies some, impresses others by its unyielding severity, and is recognized by the enlightened as a law of undeviating justice.

Personal will is a feeling caused by the working of cosmic forces through a human organism. Volition is the operation of natural law.

The human body is a vehicle (chariot) whereby universal forces are so interrupted that they produce various manifestations, psychic and physical. The process of limitation and specialization begun in Binah results in tensions that we feel. These feelings are the cause of belief in a personal will. Careful discrimination demonstrates that *the expression of will is the equilibration of opposing tensions.* This is produced by the Life-power, working in personality according to undeviating laws, mental and physical.

The letter Cheth (ח) represents the field of personality. What occurs in the field does not originate therein and is not limited to its boundaries. The fence of personal consciousness surrounds it. However, there is land outside and inside a fence. The property existed before a fence was built. The land outside is continuous with the inside. And so, the fence of personality is not separated from what is outside.

This is the essence of all transgression. It creeps into and poisons much of what passes for occult teaching. That is, the attempt to control the action of the Divine Spirit (Shin) by imposing upon it forms built up by "personal will" (Peh). This builds the Tower of Babel.

Many will-training systems, so-called Yoga, New Thought, and other metaphysical teachings endeavor to do this. They seek to impose our will upon the Cosmic Life. They teach their dupes to force Universal Consciousness to manifest their desired forms. This is real black magic, and its ultimate result is the ruin pictured by Key 16. The real magic is just the reverse.

The Magic of Light makes our world what we want by giving us the power to see that the real world is wonderful and harmonious. Reality is beyond our imagination; to perceive it is the satisfaction of every desire. Real happiness is not a mental narcotic that sends us to a dream world where we forget "harsh actualities."

It is just the opposite. It wakes us up and brings us into a state where no good or perfect gift, small or great, is withheld from us. It wakes us into a world of health and beautiful human relationships, where every moment of victory and every experience is a phase of Eternal Success. It shows us a world where work is a joy instead of wanting its completion. Hence Levi's old manuscript says that he who possesses the path of Cheth has the power to find the philosophical stone.

The consciousness we have just described cannot be counterfeited. We cannot pretend to have it because it is the perception that the real Mover, Thinker, and Actor in human personality is the Cosmic One Self symbolized by the Charioteer. The Charioteer's will is the only will. Will-power is manifested by those who are wholly receptive to that One Will.

This receptivity cannot be simulated. A person may talk about it fluently and convincingly. Their words may lead some to find the way. Yet, people cannot become genuinely receptive while working to satisfy their wants. Therefore, seek the kingdom of heaven first, and all other things will be added to you (Matthew 6:33).

The kingdom must be sought for its own sake. They who put the quest for it before all else will have all things needful added unto them. If one seeks the kingdom to get things, their real objectives are the things, not the kingdom, and they miss both.

Thus, in Key 7, the chariot is standing still. No activity of personality is personal – "I am doing nothing." Instead, the senses and organs move by the natural impulse to their appropriate objects. And the natural impulse is the outward and downward flow of the One Life. Then the seeker for light is set free from the sense of separateness. When this liberation comes, they are in harmony with the Law (Geburah) and identify with it. Then we realize it has always been the undeviating Justice that regulates every circumstance of our life.

CHAPTER 11

19th Path of Teth - ט

The Intelligence of the Secret All Spiritual Activities

The 19th Path is the Intelligence of the Secret All Spiritual Activities (Sekhel Sod Ha.Paulot Ha.ruchniot Kulam). It is the influx (18th Path) that permeates from the Supreme Blessing and the Glory of the Most High.

שכל	נקרא	תשעה	ה-נתיב
Intelligence	is called	9	The Path

כולם	ה-רוחניות	ה-פעולות	סוד
all	Spiritual(s)	the actions	secret
everyone	רוח	activities	
	Rauch		

ה-מתפשט	ה-שפע	שהוא	מפני
pervasive	influx	It is	because
permeates	abundance		
	18th Path		

ו-ה-כבוד	ה-עליונה	מהברכה	בו
& the glory	the height	blessing	from
	supreme		with

ה-מעולה			
the excellent			

180

The 19th Path is called the Intelligence of the Secret, or Intelligence of all Spiritual Activities, because an influx is spread for it from the highest benediction [or recipient] and by the noblest or supreme glory. It is the path of influx towards all Measures [Sephiroth].

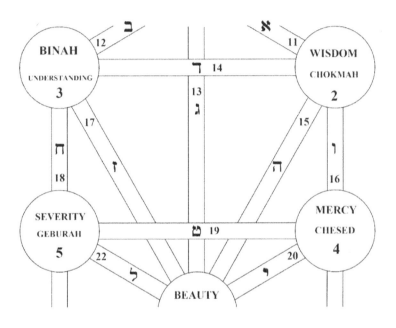

The nineteenth path of wisdom is Teth (ט), symbolized by Key 8. It is the second of the reciprocal paths uniting the Pillar of Mercy to the Pillar of Severity. It is the first of the three paths proceeding from Chesed that joins to Geburah.

The nineteenth path is called the Intelligence of the Secret of all Spiritual Activities – *Sekhel Sod Ha.Paulot Ha.ruchniot Kulam* (שכל סוד ה-פעולות ה-רוחניות כולם).

Teth ט

The two states of Divine Transcendence and Immanence involve hiddenness, symbolized by the Tet. Divine Transcendence implies, from our human perspective, a certain withdrawal from active involvement in worldly affairs. On the other hand, divine Immanence, though permeating the consciousness of all levels of Creation, must nonetheless be concealed in no small extent to endow Creation with a sense of independence and a man with free choice." – *The Hebrew Letters*, p. 143.

Teth ט – North Above

In the Tarot color scale, the nineteenth path of Teth is brilliant yellow. This is also the tint of the twelfth path (Beth, Key 1) and Tiphareth (the seat of the One Ego). The same color is assigned to Mercury and the upper surface of the Cube of Space.

On the cube, Teth (ט) is assigned to North-Above. This is the boundary where the top and the north side meet on the cube. The north face is Mars. The top is Mercury. The path of Teth is the combination of the powers of Mars and Mercury.

The connection between the nineteenth and twelfth (Beth) paths is seen in the symbols of Key 8. A woman is the Key's central figure but wears a white robe, like the Magician. Over her head is a horizontal figure 8, like the Magician. When the Tarot shows a woman, it's representing subconsciousness. The primary power of subconsciousness is memory. Thus in Key 8, illustrating the nineteenth path, the woman stands for the cosmic memory seated in Chesed. The dominant influence in the nineteenth path is recollection, and remembrance is part of the secret mentioned in the path's title.

182

Key 8 - Strength

Key 8 shows a lion, tamed by the woman and led by a chain of roses. He is a red lion. Red is the color of Geburah, the Sphere of Mars. It is at the end of the nineteenth path and the color of the northern face of the Cube.

The woman in Key 8 is the Empress, not the High Priestess. However, the Empress and High Priestess are not two. The two Keys represent two aspects of subconsciousness. Though the power of memory (Moon) dominates in Key 8, the subconscious power of generating mental imagery associated with Venus is more evident.

Secrets of the 19th Path

The prime secret of the nineteenth path is that whatever exists is a form of spiritual energy. All spiritual energy is subject to the direction and control of the form above it. The conscious imagery of humanity is a form of spiritual energy. All forms below this level are subject to its direction. Our mental imagery, in turn, is subject to the influence which descends from superconscious levels. It flows down into subconscious levels through the agency of the mind. *The mind is the mediator between that which is above and that which is below.*

Humanity is the synthesis of all cosmic activities. Human intelligence gathers all the threads of the Life-power's self-manifestation. By operating the law pictured in Key 8, human intelligence carries the cosmic life expression into manifestations beyond anything nature can manifest. By controlling the subconscious production of mental images, we can "open the lion's mouth" and bring sub-human forces under our direction.

In so doing, humanity acts as the vehicle of universal life. We may say that the universal One Self, Yekhidah in Kether, does nothing. That One Self is the ONE IDENTITY called "God" by theologians, and God is changeless. The One Self is the witness of activity but is not modified or altered by its transformations. All change and modifications are in the energy field, which revolves around the SMALL POINT at the very center of Kether. The One Self, the rider in the chariot of human personality, is free from a necessity for any endeavor. It does nothing. It has never done anything. The witness of the panorama of transformations proceeds from its mysterious power, symbolized by the woman in Key 8.

Through the right recollection or contact with the deeper levels of memory, it is possible to discover that the cosmic order is not merely a mechanism. When we learn how to listen, it speaks to us. On the mechanism of nature are written characters we can learn to read. Within us is a point of contact that reveals the meaning of an experience. No matter the appearance of an event, it has a meaning for us and may be put to productive use in what we think, say, and do.

The power at work in the nineteenth path that proceeds from the Chesed is a power related to the wisdom which sends down its influence into the fourth Sephirah through the path of Vav (The Hierophant). One part of the secret we are now studying is that the woman tames the lion because the Hierophant has instructed her.

Another part of the secret is that human life extends beyond the physical world's limits even now. Humanity is a four-dimensional being. However, few men and women are conscious of this.

184

Humans are immortal, even though millions believe they are mortals. Thus one of the practical consequences of attaining that mastery of sub-human powers, pictured by Key 8, is the liberation of humans into conscious awareness of immortality.

When we establish contact with the inner principle of wisdom, the world assumes a different appearance. Little by little, it is revealed as being beautiful and having the same essential nature as ourselves. Nothing in it is alien to us. Nothing is adverse. When we know it right, we find naught to dread but everything to accept and use.

The universe is rational. It is composed of patterns intelligible to the mind of humanity. Therefore, we must train ourselves to look for these patterns. Key 1, The Magician symbolizes the training necessary.

The ONE IDENTITY's manifesting power is grounded in the Life-power's perfect remembrance of itself and everything it has done. Because the Life-power is the central reality of every personal existence, every human can access the past's permanent, perfect record. The ONE IDENTITY's memory links all personalities, as characters in a novel are linked by the author's consciousness. The field of this memory is Chesed, from which the nineteenth path proceeds.

The nineteenth path ends in the Sphere of Mars, pictured in Key 8 as the lion. He corresponds to one of the names of the fifth Sephirah, Pachad (פחד), Fear. All our fears are variations of the fear of death. Hence we may understand that to tame the lion is to overcome that last enemy.

Here, observation and memory are active. Surface appearances lead many to suppose the absence of death would be an excellent thing. However, the dissolution of physical bodies is a necessary and benevolent manifestation of life. However, dissolution is not the cessation of human existence.

The Mars force can be directed and controlled using mental imagery. This is another aspect of the secret of the nineteenth path. The Magician represents mastery of the Mars force using mental imagery. Those who possess the nineteenth path are conscious transformers of their physical organism utilizing mental imagery. Then subconsciousness finishes the work employing the law pictured in Key 8. They deliberately plan their regeneration. They arrange a new life for themselves. They become an instrument for a higher power.

These practices affect changes in one's physical body; nobody is born an adept. Nobody succeeds in Great Work without undergoing profound personality changes. Though the One Self is indeed changeless, the mere affirmation of the One I AM's unchanging perfection will not make that perfection manifest on the physical plane.

Though inequality and injustice are apparent everywhere, these are appearances that veil the truth. Universal Justice is always in manifestation. The perfect balance of forces is maintained continually. From the beginning of this world cycle to the present moment, there has never been one slightest deviation from the operation of perfect justice. To know it is to possess the final secret of the nineteenth path.

The great secret is that we have nothing to acquire. By elimination, we perform the Great Work, symbolized in Key 8 and Key 6, by a

186

mountain in the background. We must eliminate our prejudices, hates, dislikes, and faulty opinions. How shall we accomplish this? We immerse ourselves daily and hourly, thinking that all experiences are the Lifepower working upon our personality. The Life-power molds us into a perfected vehicle. It guides us on the path to recognizing the manifestation of justice in every circumstance of our lives.

Intelligence of Will

The 20th Path is the Intelligence of Will (Sekhel HaRatzon). It is the trait from which everything is formed. Through this consciousness, everyone can know the essence of Original Wisdom.

ה-נתיב	העשרים	נקרא	שכל
The Path	20	is called	Intelligence

ה-רצון	מפני	שהוא	תכונת
the will	because	It is	attribute, trait
goodwill			
desire			

כל	ה-יצורים	כולם	ו-ב-זה
all	fabrication, form(s)	all	&-in-this
	formed	everyone	Through this

ה-שכל	כל	יודע	מציאות
consciousness	all	know	existence
		knowing	essence

ה-חכמה	ה-קדומה
Chokmah	the ancient
wisdom	original, primordial
intelligence	
science	

188

The 20th Path is called the Intelligence of Will because it is the organization of every created being, and through it, the existence of primordial knowledge becomes very known. It is the path of the mysteries of knowledge.

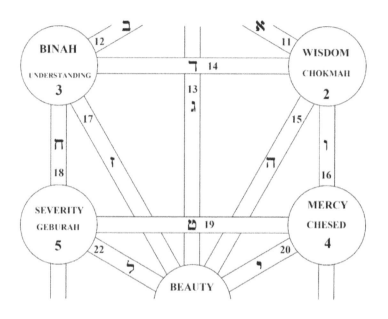

Ratzon רצון

Ratzon (רצון) means *will, goodwill, wish, desire; acceptance; favor*, and *grace*. So the idea associated with this word suggests receptivity. So we feel in our bodies as the "will" power is the light-force surging through our bloodstream, nerve, and tissue.

Rawtzone will, by its four letters, represent radiant energy or fire (Resh), air (Tzaddi); earth (Vav); and water (Nun). The occult significance of the word relates to the idea of a synthesis of the four elements, which is none other than the One Reality, the Ancient of Days represented by the Hermit, and customarily designated by the Divine Name Jehovah.

189

"In the service of G-d, the 'pathway' is the ability to contract and direct one's energy in a concentrated and purposeful way. Finding the 'pathway,' one's direction in life, depends upon the ability to subdue one's worldly desires and passions and to humble one's ego. This is the act of contraction, *tzimtzum*, by which one enters the consciousness of the present moment, the point of 'suspended animation' – continual re-creation." *The Hebrew Letters*, p. 156

Cube of Space – North Below

On the Cube of Space, this path is at the northern face's junction with the lower face. The direction assigned to it is North-Below. The twentieth path's secret is the Mars force's operation (north) at the subconscious levels (below).

The power at work in the twentieth path is another phase of the nineteenth. It has its source in the first Sephirah, whence it descends to Chokmah through the path of Aleph. From Chokmah, it descends to Chesed through the path of Vav. The Limitless light, concentrated in Kether, specialized as the masculine and paternal life-force, Chaiah, in Chokmah, and working in Chesed as Beneficence.

The Hermit

Thus the Hermit is an older man, shown in profile, to indicate Yekhidah in Kether. On his head is a blue Yod (׳), the color of Gimel (ג), and the High Priestess, indicating that subconsciousness is active in the twentieth path. Yod has its top point in Kether and its body in Chokmah. Chokmah's color is grey, the same as the Hermit's robe. The Hermit's gaze is directed backward along the path and symbolizes memory, the unique quality attributed to Chesed. Finally, it is a night scene, and the darkness is an ancient symbol for all things about subconscious forces and activities.

The star in the Hermit's hexagonal lantern is the macrocosmic star. The hexagram is the Shield of David or Shield of Love. This is mahgen David (מגן דוד), and its value, 107, is the sum of Ab (אב, 3) Aima (אימא, 52) and Ben (בן, 52). These are the names of the Qabalistic Trinity, Father (Chokmah), Mother (Binah), and Son (Tiphareth). By Latin Cabala, 107 is Christus, Christ, and Lux Domini's value, Light of the Lord.

The One Ego seated in Tiphareth is the focal point of the Tree of Life. The sixth Sephirah is the apex of a down-pointing triangle whose other angles are Ab, the Father, and Aima, the Mother. Finally, the One Ego is one with the paternal life-force in Chokmah and the maternal Divine Soul, Neshamah, in Binah. The unity linking these three aspects of the One Reality is the single substance – LIGHT – the light of stars and humanity's inner light.

What we feel in our bodies as the power called "will" is the surge of the light-force through the bloodstream and nerve and tissue. The hexagram is a synthesis of the alchemical symbols of the four elements, and the letters *ratzon* (רצון) represent the same four elements.

Resh (ר) – Fire
Tzaddi (צ) – Air
Vav (ו) – Earth
Nun (ן) - Water

The elements are the four phases in manifesting one fundamental reality – LIGHT.

Will

What the ignorant misinterpret as independent, personal free will, the wise declare to be something like a tropism (the turning of an organism in a particular direction in response to an external stimulus). As moths fly towards light, so do we turn, by an irresistible impulse, toward the Inner Light symbolized by the Hermit's lantern. While we are far from the one goal, we suppose ourselves to be choosing our objectives. When we near our destination, we know we have no "will of our own."

Human personality is a synthesis of all cosmic processes. Humanity summarizes all that preceded us and is the point of departure for developing a new creature. The natural human is the seed of the spiritual human. When we understand the processes that have brought him as far as the natural man, we may consciously and intentionally utilize these processes to take us farther. They who have grasped this truth echo Jesus' declaration, "I have no will, save to do the will of Him that sent me."

Not by attempting to force nature into our mold, but rather by identifying ourselves with her perfect order, shall we find the freedom we seek. The real magical will is perfect obedience. Not by changing nature, but by discovering her laws and our place in her operation, do we enter into freedom, power, and happiness.

Daily practice of the thought that a higher intelligence guides personal life, daily remembrance that nobody can do anything for themselves and daily endeavor to approach conditions and circumstances from this point of view are the training's fundamentals.

Those who want to develop the magical will must seek to clarify their vision of what lies beyond the heights of present human attainment. Again and again, we remind ourselves that Principle is never bound by precedent. We must open ourselves to the influx of the ONE LIGHT. Our daily, hourly quest must be to make ourselves receptive to the vision which comes from above.

In so doing, we are making deliberate, conscious choices. However, we understand it as the drive of the ONE WILL. The greater part of our training aims at never forgetting the true meaning of these feelings we share with all humanity. Thus, the twentieth path takes us from Tiphareth to Chesed – from intellectual recognition of the central One Ego's true nature to complete identification with the cosmic memory.

Understand that the cosmic process is meditation. The Hermit is in meditation, and his isolation corresponds to the outcome of meditation, described by the Sanskrit term Kaivalya, meaning "alone."

The Life-power is conscious energy flowing through a succession of forms that are, without exception, related to a particular object. Every cycle of the Life-power's self-expression has a definite objective. From the beginning of the cycle to its completion, the aim is never forgotten.

We do not share the Life-power's perception of its objective until we have identified ourselves with the unceasing flow of conscious energy. Later, we obtain the beatific vision of the "far-off divine event" as a present reality. This comes through meditation.

This perception leads us to a new type of awareness. This is dimly apprehended in modern teachings having to do with the so-called Fourth Dimension.

This experience includes first-hand knowledge that human personality is a center of expression for the MIND that constitutes, frames, and composes the universe's laws. There is, in each of us, acting through our brain, an expression of the power that rules and regulates the forces of nature. This power is pictured as The Emperor and The Hermit.

In our day-to-day experience, all our exercise of willpower is directed toward overcoming appearances of limitation. Even when we seem to will evil, it is true. The drive behind even the most heinous crimes is always the desire for freedom.

Whatever they may be, behind all appearances is a Perfect Law's operation, having Beauty for its foundation. If we see ugliness, it is because we do not see right. If we will evil, we are suffering from a kind of insanity. Thus Eliphas Levi says that black magic is organized madness.

True Magic is in the Will

Levi says all true magic is in the will. Yet, reading or listening to a human teacher cannot obtain this knowledge. Instead, we must listen profoundly to the Inner Voice's instruction to know the twentieth path of wisdom's inner meaning. This listening is an active state of consciousness, a throwing of the whole mind into the form of intense, expectant receptivity.

The possessor of this twentieth path is said: "to be acquainted with the laws of perpetual motion and to be in a position to demonstrate the quadrature of the circle." This statement has nothing to do with making a perpetual motion machine nor with the vain endeavor to construct a square whose area shall be the same as a given circle (See Appendix 5 for my vain attempt to square the circle.)

The possessor of the path of Yod is "acquainted with the laws of perpetual motion" because this path leads to perfect identification with the One Conscious Energy and knowledge of its laws. This is because the infinite whirling motion of the Limitless Light is the actual perpetual motion. Therefore, they who know the secret of the Intelligence of Will possess full knowledge of this energy and its laws.

Thus they can demonstrate or manifest control of circumstance through their union with the One Will-Power. This pure spiritual will is the perfect circle of Divine Life. Therefore, those in union with it express the perfect order in everything they do.

That order is symbolized by the number 4 and by the square. It is the perfect order of Chesed, descending into Tiphareth through the twentieth path of wisdom.

They who ascend through the twentieth path to the Grade of Exempt Adept can make this occult demonstration of the squaring of the circle. They do nothing of themselves because they are unobstructed channels for Divine Beneficence, perfect manifestations of the Heavenly Order.

CHAPTER 12

21st Path of Kaph - כ

Seeking Intelligence

The 21st Path is the Desirous Quest Intelligence (Sekhel HaChafutz HaMevukash). It receives the divine influx to bless all, everyone. (Also translated, Seeking and Delightful Intelligence).

ה-נתיב	אחד	ו-עשרים	נקרא
The Path	1	and 20	is called

שכל	ה-חפץ	ה-מבוקש	מפני
Intelligence	wish, desire	to ask, desire	because
	delight	seek, to search	

שהוא	מקבל	שפע	ה-אלהות
It is	receives	influx	divinity
	accepted	18th Path	divine

כדי	ל-חשפיע	מברכת	ל-כל
in order to	to influence	bless	to all
to	to bestow	ברק	
		to bless	

הנמצאים	כולם		
found	all, everyone		
available			

The 21st Path is called the Intelligence of Delight of the Desired Matter because it receives the divine influence so that it shall penetrate, by its blessing, every existing thing.

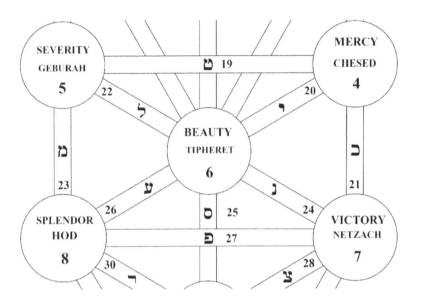

Kaph כ

"The three lines of the kaf [כ] relate to the three properties of the superconscious: simple and absolute faith, sublime pleasure in the experience of unity with G-d, and superconscious desire to dedicate one's life to fulfilling G-d's Will. These properties are called "the three heads of the crown," *Keter*. The highest of the heads, simple faith, corresponds to *Keter,* meaning "to wait," as in (כתר לי זעיר), "*wait* for me a little." This implies that faith entails the patience and confidence that G-d's ultimate good in His Divine intention for each individual soul, together with all of Creation, will in time be fulfilled." *The Hebrew Letters*, p. 171.

Desirous Quest

Mevukash (מבוקש) is from a root *bee.kaysh* (בקש), meaning to ask, beg, wish, desire, claim, seek; to require, request, demand; to search; to intend, aim at, seek and search.

Chafutz (חפץ) means to wish, want, desire, find pleasure in, have affection for, willingly, with pleasure, gladly.

Like all personal activities, our quest for abundance is a response to the descending influence of Life-power. We seek because what we seek is really within us, and whatever we gain is a recollection of what the One Identity already has in store for us.

Key 10, The Wheel of Fortune

Chesed, the 4th path of wisdom, is the Sphere of Jupiter. The 21st Path of Kaph is assigned to Jupiter. Finally, the Tree of Life is the only place where the Sephirah projects energy like itself.

Letter Name Kaph כף

Kaph means palm of the hand and is used in Job 36:32 as a metaphor for dark clouds. "With clouds (כף), he covers the light and commands lighting to hit its mark.

Rabbi Yitzchak Ginsburgh adds, "Who is the mighty one? He who suppresses his evil inclination." In the Zohar and Chassidut, this power to suppress evil is referred to as it**kaf**ia, (אתכפיא), from the root kaf (כף)."

199

The importance of the right discrimination in distinguishing the character of desires cannot be over-emphasized. Exercising such discrimination requires alertness and honesty in appraising one's motives. We must recognize the overshadowing presence of superconsciousness and deliberately deliver subconsciousness from bondage to our conscious thinking. Our expectation is fulfilled when we expect subconsciousness to respond to the influence of superconsciousness. When we act on the instruction that comes from above, we make ourselves more aware of guidance. To be a Qabalist is to be receptive.

We who are aspirants to illumination are like the invisible travelers toiling up the path over which the Hermit sheds light from his lantern. Entering the Desirous Quest's path, we have a vague notion about what we seek; something is missing. We are prone to think that all would be well if we possessed certain things or had different circumstances. As we continue to seek, we get brief flashes of the Inner Light. In time, we realize that desire is a *longing to be* rather than the wish to have. We understand that the desire to be is the Life-power's way of revealing what we are. The Way to Liberation is the path of discovery, leading to a full perception of the One Self's true nature.

It is a path or method that alters our bodies. Illumination is a consequence of cellular changes. The occult path does not lead out of this world into purely metaphysical regions. Practical occultism is not escapism. Those who succeed must keep their feet on the ground. The physical plane is as spiritual as any other. To think ill of it, to neglect it – this is the evil fruit of the error of separateness.

Adepts have bodies different from the unenlightened. The chemistry of their blood is altered. Their nerve currents move in another fashion than ordinary human beings. Brain cell structures are changed. Thus one part of the secret of the path of Desirous Quest is the transformations in the physical body.

These transformations are not mere matters of diet, exercise, breathing, or posture. In our day, there are systems for "self-development" based on the idea that one can be superman by selecting the right foods.

What we eat does make a difference. How we sit, stand, and use our lungs are important also. Yet we shall never reach the twenty-first path's goal if we suppose success to be a matter of calories and vitamins, bodily contortions, or a breathing exercise.

The balance of our interior stars requires meditation. Nobody succeeds in meditation that has a lukewarm desire for freedom. Meditation, especially in its early stages, is hard work. It must persist for some time before any striking results are attained. We must seek righteousness and remain steadfast in meditation until we taste its fruits. Thus perseverance is another secret of the path of the Desirous Quest.

A third is courage. To develop this, we must face difficulties and learn to solve problems. Silly systems of *meta-fizzling* insist that we must never admit we have problems or give a moment's thought to failure, poverty, or disease. They contend this encourages negativity. In truth, they are evading issues. To affirm the "goodness of ALL" is to speak truly enough. Affirmations are useful for one reason – to give us the strength to face our problems boldly because we are confident we have the power to turn challenges into opportunities. To stop with the affirmation, to turn ourselves into talking machines repeating statements, is the sin of vain repetition. What we need is to use daily that day's "sufficient evil."

This means keeping awake now. It means interpreting the present experiences as particular dealings of the Divine Spirit with our souls. That Spirit led the greatest adept into the wilderness to be tempted. Day after day, it subjects us to the same essential tests. To dread the future is supremely unintelligent. To refuse to face the appearance of evil in the present is even worse.

The illumined mind lives in eternity; NOW is the only human word designating this eternity. NOW is a good time. NOW is the day of liberation. Guidance comes NOW, or not at all. Although every human is always under direction, we know it to be active NOW whenever we are aware of it.

The path of Desirous Quest is associated through Kaph (כ) with Jupiter (וְ). Jupiter is pictured in Key 7 by the wheels of the chariot. There are two wheels instead of the single wheel pictured in Key 10. It symbolizes that when the twenty-first path's influence is effective in our lives, it must be felt subconsciously and consciously. It is not enough to have an intellectual perception of the truth that we receive the divine influence and partake of the blessing it distributes to all modes of being through this path. Such perception is necessary, but it is not sufficient. It must permeate our subconsciousness and be built by subconscious activities into our bodies. This is one reason for the emphasis on meditation. Truth must be printed indelibly on subconsciousness so that we never forget its principles. Only then will it bear fruit in our lives.

Subconsciousness is the transformer of our physical vehicles. It is not the ultimate cause of the transformation which brings us to the end of Desirous Quest's path. The power is superconscious. Subconsciousness is the agency through which this power works.

Self-consciousness initiates the processes which bring the required changes. However, self-consciousness does not affect the changes more than a gardener makes plants grow. He watches his garden, cultivates, and weeds it. The work of self-consciousness is to realize the rationality of Ageless Wisdom and manage thought and feeling.

All occult training systems begin by instructing the aspirant what to expect as a consequence of their practice. The words of the wise must be studied. But, impossible as it is to express the more subtle forms of spiritual experience, Jesus declared, "The seed is the word."

After the seed is planted by reading and listening to teachers, concentration and meditation practices come. These aim at reducing conscious thought to a minimum. Never do they seek to make the mind a blank. Mastery of thought includes the power to stop interference from thoughts unrelated to the primary purpose. The best way to accomplish this is by paying attention to the *particular knowledge* about which one is meditating. Truth must be printed indelibly on subconsciousness so that we never forget its principles. Then it may bear fruit in our lives.

The twenty-first path descends from Chesed, the seat of memory. It has a great deal to do with the practice of remembering. Since this path is associated with Jupiter, to possess this path is to tap into cosmic memory. We become aware of cosmic processes' essential knowledge stored in the Jupiter center or solar plexus. From meditation, we gain insight into our place in the cosmic order. We penetrate the veil of apparent mechanism and see the universe as a living organism. When we are proficient in this kind of practice, we experience cosmic consciousness.

Yet this is never known by those who content themselves with optimistic affirmations about the Life-power's goodness. Buddha did not seek liberation while he was in his palace harem and protected against every sign and sound which might make him aware of sorrow, poverty, sickness, and death. The Illuminati are men and women of sorrow and acquainted with grief. How else could they be Masters of Compassion?

In their crude forms, all our desires are variations or rebellions against some apparent bondage. The verb "to want" is sufficient proof. When any restriction upon our freedom confronts us, we are tempted to accept that restriction as a reality.

We fall and worship the devil whenever we yield to this temptation. We deny the possibility of better economics and politics. We give the lie that human nature is what it is. We cannot expect anything better. We avoid evil and resort to expedients to palliate evil because we accept the lie that humanity is the slave of circumstance. The twenty-first path's possessors face the adversary boldly and see through the appearances of evil to the glorious truth they veil.

The adept who is Lord of the Path of Kaph *can change into gold, not only all metals but also the earth itself and even the refuse of the earth.* The last phrase in this statement is a masterpiece of subtlety. The "refuse of the earth" is the same as the "Stone refused by the builders." What sense-bound materialism overlooks, and refuses to incorporate, becomes the pinnacle stone of the temple of enlightened human personality. It is the conscious recognition of the One Ego's identity in man with the Indivisible One Self, Yekhidah.

This recognition changes the *metals* of alchemy, the *interior stars,* into celestial gold, like the city in Revelations. This is the gold of spiritual enlightenment, the Transparent Jewel of Perfect realization of the Divine Order.

22ⁿᵈ Path of Lamed - ל

Faithful Intelligence

The 22ⁿᵈ Path is Faithful Intelligence (Sekhel Ne'eman). It causes spiritual powers to multiply. The Spiritual Ones are drawn close through it, and all find shelter in its shadow.

ה-נתיב	שנים	ו-עשרים	נקרא
The Path	2	20	is called

שכל	נאמן	מפני	שבו
Intelligence	faithful Loyal, firm	because	It is

מתרבים	כחות	ה-רוחניות	כדי
multiply	power, force strength	spiritual(s)	through it

להיותם	קרובים	ל-כל	ה-יתלוננים
to be	close, relation near, at hand	to all	dwell

ב-צילו			
in his shadow shelter			

The 22nd Path is called the Faithful Intelligence because spiritual virtues have been deposited into its hands and nurtured so that they shall be close to those who live under its shadow.

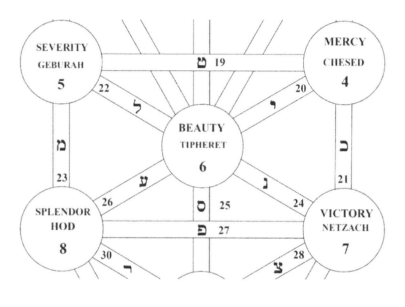

Lamed ל

Yod is the smallest letter, and Lamed is the largest. It is the only letter that goes above the upper bound of the other letters. Lamed is called the "flying tower." It symbolizes our desire and aspiration to understand the world we live in.

Lamed means both to teach and to learn. Rabbi Ginsburgh adds, "He who learns to teach is granted the ability to learn and teach; he who learns in order to *do* is granted the ability to learn, teach, guard and do."

Ne'eman (נאמן) is from the root *amen* (אמן). It means *to be found true, trustworthy, firm*; *to confirm*; *faithfulness, loyalty,* and *so be it*. Amen also means *artist, expert,* or *master craftsman*.

Key 11 - Justice

The sword in the right hand of Justice in Key 11 (the path of Lamed) corresponds to Mars. If Key 11 is placed on the twenty-second path, the sword is nearest the beginning of the path in Geburah (Sphere of Mars). Also, the scales are on the side nearest the end of the path. They are of gold, the metal of the Sun, of which Tiphareth is the sphere.

Saturn is exalted in Libra. In the Great Work, the serpent's power is exalted or lifted by sublimation. It is raised from the Saturn center at the base of the spine and is combined with the Mars energy active in the interior star next above the Saturn center. Thus the hilt of the sword of Justice is a T-cross. It symbolizes the Saturn force at the base of the spine, and when this is lifted, it elevates the blade of the sword, representing the Mars force.

This leads to illumination, which inspires no fear in the creatures of the sub-human kingdoms. The ignorant and evil fear them because they misunderstand adepts. Their works of power frighten onlookers. Their command of circumstances is a consequence of being a free channel for the One Free Will. The Will centered in human personality manifests as the equilibrating power that establishes the undeviating Justice of Universal Law.

Volition

The twenty-second path is the volition drive. It is fiery and Martian but also the Pranic force, partaking in the spiritual power of air or breath.

Its urge is toward increase, and because increase is growth, the twenty-second path is related to the reproductive drive. The Tree of Life shows the twenty-second path in the upper half of a line crossing the Tree from Geburah to Netzach, with Tiphareth at its center. The lower part of this line, corresponding to Nun (נ), and Key 13, is the continuation of the path of Lamed.

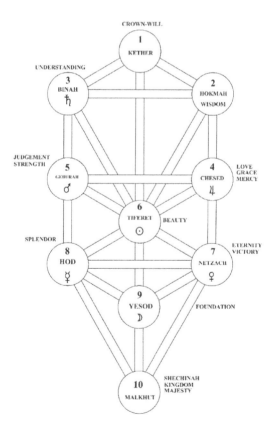

In medical astrology, Lamed rules the kidneys. In ancient times, it was thought the kidneys were related to reproduction. Hence *kolyaw* (כוליא) is translated as *kidney* and *gonad.*

On top of the kidneys are adrenal glands that are related to Mars. The chemicals they pour into the bloodstream stimulate and intensify muscle tone. These organs affect our ability to perform works requiring volition. Our work brings about changes in our environment. Therefore the twenty-second path is the beginning of that descent of power, which shows completion in the symbolism in Key 13.

When we will, we aim at change. Every strong volition is a practical demonstration of the delusion that any human is an independent, separate personality. The magical will is not the false self-will of those seeking to impose their "own way" on others or circumstances. Eliphas Levi calls it the "will of intelligent beings," and those who merit this description are the ruling minority of the human race. They are true adepts whose will is the law because it is identified with the absolute Justice attributed to Geburah.

The outlook of such men and women is different. Their objectives are beyond the range of the vision of the ordinary, earth-bound *genus homo.* The world laughs at their ideas and thinks their dreams of a better world order are foolish and impractical enthusiasm. Yet the foolishness of seers is the hope of humanity, and to it, we may trace every step in society's progress.

Seers know first-hand that the life of humanity includes a consciousness above our intellectual level. They live by the guidance which comes to them from within and from above. They know that this guidance from a higher level is the birthright of every human being. Their instruction proclaims this birthright and is founded on their knowledge of the correct way to use its liberating power.

All this instruction has, for its basis, that people are not the thinker, speaker, or actor. Every thought, word, and deed is the operation of universal powers and laws, known and unknown, taking form through human beings or another active center of expression for the One Life. This is not fatalism, but discriminating between the personality and the One Self. The One Self is the Indivisible One, the originating principle of the universe. Personality is dependent, conditioned, and determined. The One Self is free and is the conditioner and determiner of the functions and activities of character.

Those who see the truth can make new combinations by exercising creative imagination. Humanity is the instrument for the modification of the cosmos. Human personality is the *indispensable agency* whereby the Life-power completes the Great Work. All work, including the Great Work, is related to the twenty-second path. Key 11 symbolizes this: "Equilibrium is the secret of the Great Work."

This equilibrium is affected by human life through subconsciousness. Thus the central figure in Key 11 is the same as the High Priestess in Key 2. The pomegranates on the veil behind the High Priestess are symbols of the increase of spiritual powers mentioned in the text concerning the path of Lamed. Their pattern resembles the Tree of Life because Sephiroth summarizes all spiritual powers.

Subconsciousness is the agency of the transformation. However, the Great Work is under the supervision of Key 4. In the Tarot Tableau, Key 4 is above Key 11, in the vertical row, with Key 18

211

at the bottom. Therefore, we must be well grounded in theory before attempting the practice. Poor reasoners never succeed in the operations of the twenty-second path.

The transformations of personality are accomplished under the direction of self-consciousness. They are the results of clear and definite intention and long-continued practice.

The Rosicrucian *Confessio* says, "Flesh and blood cannot inherit the kingdom of God." Therefore, every seeker for illumination must do their work and bring about their release from the bonds of error.

Yet the mystery teaching says the sense of personal effort is an illusion. However, *by no means should individual effort be abandoned.* On the contrary, the work whereby humanity is set free feels like a personal exercise of the power of will, which is seated in Geburah. Still, this work's consequence is the new creature, whose mind is freed from the delusion. Hence there is no trace of self-importance in a true adept. He has become the Little Child, a term used to describe the highest human attainment. He is free from the burden of false responsibilities and the limitations of conventions and opinions that are the mental fetters worn by most humans.

Such a regenerated personality has tremendous power over sub-human modes of the Life-power's self-expression. Key 11 represents this power through the balanced scales in the woman's left hand. The possessors of the twenty-second path's power are mentally and emotionally poised, and the result of their work establishes equilibrium in their surroundings. They are free from fear, and thus they inspire no fear. In the most literal sense, they can subdue the most ferocious animals and "pronounce the words which paralyze and charm serpents." They can master the wild beasts in their environment because they have subdued their counterparts in their nature. They can charm serpents because the twenty-second path's work has made them masters of the coiled serpent power in their organism.

CHAPTER 13

23rd Path of Mem - מ

Sustaining Intelligence

The 23rd Path is Sustaining Intelligence (Sekhel Kayam). It is the power sustaining all the Sephiroth.

נקרא	ו-עשרים	שלשה	ה-נתיב
is called	20	3	The Path

שהוא	מפני	קיום	שכל
It is	because	sustaining subsistence	Intelligence

ה-ספירות	ל-כל	קיום	כח
Sephiroth numbers	to all	sustaining subsistence	power, strength

The 23rd Path is called the Established Intelligence because it is the virtue of consistency for all numerations [Sephiroth].

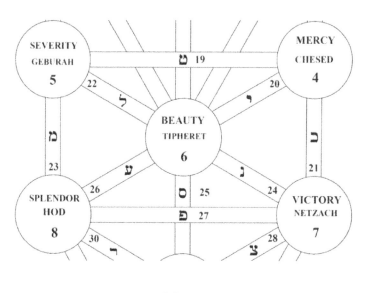

Mem מ

The open Mem (מ) is a fountain whose water runs above ground. The final closed Mem (ם) is a sealed underground fountain. The final form of Mem resembles a womb, which is the fountain of life.

The path from Kether to Chokmah is considered a flowing stream of wisdom and a Torah metaphor.

"Wisdom (Torah) is a tree of life to those who embrace her; happy are those who hold her tightly." – Proverbs 3:18.

Stable Intelligence

Kayam (קיום) means *existence, approval, confirmation, observance, survival,* and *subsistence.* From the root, *k'yam* (קים) means *permanence, duration, durability,* and *everlastingness.*

The Hanged Man

The Hanged Man is a synthesis of the whole Tarot. With the final Mem (ם) placed with Tav (ת) at the center of the Cube of Space, they spell *toom* (תם), signifying the ultimate attainment and ultimate perfection.

The Hanged Man has white hair, like the Hermit and the Emperor. However, the state of perfect stability of mind he symbolizes cannot be arrived at without reasoning. It requires the secret operations over which the Hermit presides. These are the subtle changes in the body's chemistry that occur in the body's Virgo region. The main achievement is the seedless Samadhi pictured by Key 12. It is the vision symbolized by the gaze of the Fool.

Vision, not thought. Direct perception, not speculation. The Eye Divine, not the eyes of sense. On the Fool's wallet is an eye in the position usually occupied by a lock. The Fool looks back, up the path of Aleph (א), toward the Supreme Height, the Innermost Center. When the soul's eye is single, the whole body is filled with the light of the SINGLE WHITE BRILLIANCE. Then all old things pass away. The lower mind's conceptions are reversed, and the wisdom of this world is seen as folly.

The ONE is responsible for everything; darkness, light, evil, and peace. It depends on where we look. Liberation comes when we face the Source instead of looking toward the phenomenal, illusionary outward appearances. This is the Great Reversal pictured by Key 12, and the secret of stability is in it.

216

Concentration is the beginning of the practical work, which makes one a possessor of the twenty-third path. The impersonality suggested by Key 12 is a direct consequence of the seer's realization that their personality is symbolized by Key 7, the Chariot. Prolonged concentration and meditation are necessary for a person to reverse their ideas on free will and separate existence. Then they experience the complete dependence symbolized by the Hanged Man.

The Hanged man has glory around his head caused by the sublimation or rising of the Kundalini energy. This is called Hatha Yoga in Oriental teachings.

Theosophists condemn this as leading toward black magic. With some justice, they say that body control turns the spiritual eye away from reality toward illusion because the body is an illusion. Some say that Hatha Yoga practices never attain a good result; they say too much. However dangerous they may be when attempted by uninstructed persons under the direction of a competent teacher, some of these practices prove to be of considerable value. Yet where in the Western world can you find such a teacher? How do you judge a prospective Guru's competence? Indeed, no self-advertising "Swami" will be qualified. The Rishis and other Asian traders on European ignorance have nothing of real value to offer.

More importantly, the same results, including the sublimation of the serpent-power, are attainable by fixing the inner eye on the vision of the ONE One Self.

OBTW.

217

If you want to learn more about Kundalini, I recommend *Kundalini Exposed* by Santata Gamana. That's not his real name. He prefers to remain anonymous. Mr. Gamana has a series of books that are no-nonsense practices without all the dogma surrounding Kundalini.

Back to the text.

Samadhi

The twenty-third path is the third descent from Kether along the north side of the Tree of Life. Thus it is a consequence of the Magician. A seer in Samadhi does not lose self-consciousness. They can descend into ordinary modes of human life at will. They may detach attention from the phantasmagoria of sensation, but they can resume their place among ordinary humans whenever they will.

Patanjali states the secret of the twenty-third path in the Yoga Sutras: "Yoga is the restriction of the mind-stuff fluctuations." The mind stuff is Water. The Tarot begins with the robe of the High Priestess. Next is the waterfall in the Empress' garden. (Note that the number of Key 12 reduces to 3, the number of the Empress.) The "fluctuations of the mind-stuff" are states of consciousness brought into being by subconscious activity in generating mental images. In Samadhi, these fluctuations are restricted. There is an unbroken flow of knowledge in a particular object.

The associative functions of subconsciousness are limited by concentration. In Key 12, the Hanged Man (suspended mind) is supported by a gallows in the form of Tav (ת), attributed to Saturn, symbolizing limitation. The Hanged Man is the "adept bound by

218

his engagements." The engagements are like a wheel within a piece of machinery. Then, we link with the engine, like engaging an automobile's clutch. The results of yoga are the consequence of the person practicing control of the fluctuations of the mind stuff.

In the earlier stages of the work, this intention has continually to be recollected. A continuous flow of knowledge in a particular object is impossible unless the object is remembered and kept in mind.

Lux Mundi – 106

The *Ars Notaria* is the art of reading and understanding the signs and characters of nature. The *Confessio Fraternatatis*, Chapter 6, says, "God has inscribed upon the mechanism of the world, and which He repeats through the mutations of Empires." The signs and characters may be discerned in every kingdom of nature. Seers read and understand them, for seers, through the Single Eye-opening, are filled with the "Light of the World."

In Latin, light of the world is *Lux Mundi*, and numerically equal to 104, which is the value of *Ars Notaria*. The Lux Mundi is shown in Key 12 as the radiance around the Hanged Man's head. To have the Ars Notaria is to read what the Rosicrucian texts call *Book M* or *Sepher Mem* (ספר מים) with the enumeration of 430, equivalent to *m'sah.p'reem* (מספרים), the verb *declare*. It's used in the nineteenth Psalm: "The heavens declare the glory of God." Ha-Shamain, "the heavens," is the numeral equivalent to Neshamah, the Divine Soul seated in Binah. The Illuminati are recipients, through intuition, of the perfect understanding of the cosmic order behind the heavens that they can read the "one, only book" from which all secrets are to be learned.

Seers like these are light-bearers for humanity. They plant the seeds of great civilizations. They are not like the "planners"– each with a "one and only" scheme for a New Deal, or a Fair Deal, or some other shuffle, and all quarreling bitterly with one another. On the contrary, the Knowers of the PLAN have been in perfect agreement through the ages. They have one message, doctrine, and practice.

The aim of practical occultism is the production of a *new creature*. The New Order in society will constitute members who are genuinely enlightened men and women who will be the real governors. They will govern by their superior insight and the proper, non-coercive exercise of superior powers. They will be able to modify the minds of their contemporaries for the good of all. Thus, no matter who are the apparent heads of government, the actual rulers will be enlightened seers.

Here we come close to a great mystery. Despite present appearances, an inner circle of enlightened adepts is now and has been for thousands of years, the World Government, not merely of nations. Because they are wise, they know how to manage the masses of ignorant humanity. Out of all the turmoil of false patriotism, false economics, and the wars and misery resulting from widespread ignorance, an advance toward the New Order has been made. Because they are wise, they know how to take advantage of times and seasons. They rush nothing and are never in a hurry. They look forward confidently to the perfect realization of the Eternal Splendor and know how to bring it to pass.

The false order is breaking up. It will make way for the worldwide establishment of what was begun in America in 1776. Where there is no vision, the people perish, but in the world today, there is a real vision of a better society, and because of it, the suffering billions of the human race will soon enjoy freedom as they have not yet dared to dream, much less expect.

Imaginative Intelligence

The 24th Path is *Imaginative Intelligence* (Sekhel Dimyoni). It gives form to the imaginations of all Living Creatures.

ה-נתיב	ארבעה	ו-עשרים	נקרא
The Path	4	& 20	is called

שכל	דמיוני	מפני	שהוא
Intelligence	imaginative resemblance	because	It is

נותן	דמות	ל-כל	ה-דמיונים
gives provides	likeness image	of all	imaginations

נבראים
Living Creatures

Latin Commentary

The 24th Path is called Imaginative Intelligence because it grants similarity to each affinity among the created things.

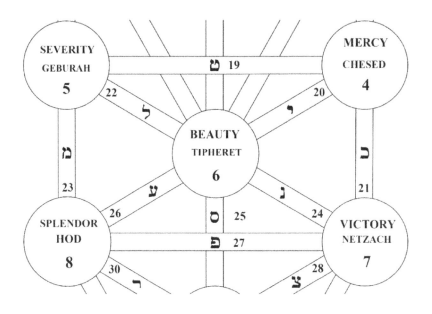

Letter Nun נ

The Letter Nun is a pictograph of sprouted seed. In Ancient Egypt, Nun is the primordial waters' where the *benben stone* arose as dry land.

Letter Name Nun – 106

The text says, "gives a *form* to the imaginations." The twenty-ninth path of Qoph (ק) is associated with the *form and growth* of physical bodies. This suggests that the imaginations of Nun's path are given physical form in the path of Qoph.

The Letter name Nun (נון) is 106, the number of the years of Brother C.R.'s life, a personification of the One Ego.

223

Dimyoni (דמיוני) means *imaginary, illusory, fictitious, chimerical, exaggerated*, and *fanciful*. It is from the root *dee.mohn* meaning, *resemblance, similitude, imagination, fantasy*, and *likeness*. All these shades of meaning suggest something that is formed in the mind.

Dimyoni can be divided into two words:

1. *dam* (דם) meaning blood.

2. *heh.vee.yon*, (חביון) meaning *hidden treasure*.

Therefore, the twenty-fourth path involves modifications of the blood and its secret properties.

Dimyoni is numerically 120. This is the number of years Brother C.R. laid in his crypt before it was opened. The vault is "a single compendium of the whole universe."

120 is 3 x 40. Forty is the number of weeks for human gestation and suggests a time of darkness before birth. It rained 40 days and nights in the biblical flood story, a symbol of test and trial before the new birth. The letter name Samekh (סמך) is also 120, and this is the Experimental or Testing Intelligence.

The kind of test is revealed in the number 120, which is the summation of numbers from 1 to 15. Therefore Key 15, The Devil is the adversary, teaches us how to play the game with skill – the Regenerating Intelligence.

Fear of Death

One of the results of concentration and meditation is eradicating the fear of death. Isis-Urania lifts her veil for none but immortals. The two Rosicrucian manifestoes (*Fama* and *Confessio Fraternitatis*) address their readers as *mortals*, implying that the authors knew themselves to be immortals. They who succeed in the Great Work overcome the fear of death. Yoga doctrine says it is the same as the will-to-live.

Buddha taught the same thing. He told his disciples to eradicate the thirst for life. He meant getting rid of the fear of death, and to help his disciples do this, he set tasks in meditation that seem horrible to Western minds, accustomed to ignoring death. Thus the author of Buddhist Meditation says:

"The meditation upon the corpse, frequently practiced in the Orient, seems unsuitable (in any of its ten forms) for Western students. It would be likely to awaken an aesthetic disgust or to seem grotesque. It is supposed to bring about detachment from the lure of the flesh. The living body is also considered perpetually disintegrating, for certain cells are dying, while others are being born."

What appears to be a positive mental attitude, the will-to-live is only a rationalization of death's fear. Whatever will cure this is good. However, it must include courageous facing of death until the significance of the dissolution of physical bodies is understood. One cannot meditate on what one ignores or evades. The fear of death is eradicated by understanding what death is and its benefits. The writer of these lessons can testify that after practicing all ten Buddhist meditations on the corpse, he found the results neither grotesque nor disgusting. On the contrary, his experience with these meditations rid his mind of the fear of death.

225

The skeleton in Key 13 represents the framework or basis of all motion. The same skeleton is concealed within the dancer's body, the central figure of Key 21. The dance of life is the cosmic manifestation of the same power symbolized as the reaper in Key 13.

Key 13 is a symbol of the will-to-live. It is the link between the One Ego and the desire nature. All our desires are variants of the will-to-live. No matter what forms our desires may take, what we all want is a more abundant life. We arrive at freedom from desire when we grasp that our desires are intimations that we already possess that we seem to lack.

The twenty-fourth path is the One Ego's power to project mental images. Desires tend to take form in some physical activity, and every physical action is a little death. Practical occultism tends to put out the fires of desire and end the generation of diverse mental images leading to action.

When we realize that human personality never acts, the chariot comes to a standstill, as in Key 7. When one is fully absorbed, through Samadhi, one identifies with the ACTIONLESS, the One Self. The one becomes like the sphinx in Key 10. The wheel of manifestation turns, but the One Self remains immobile.

The wise want nothing because they realize their perfect union with the Possessor of ALL. "All power is given to me of my Father."

Note the present tense. The will-to-live ceases when we find within ourselves the fountain of Limitless Life. Tasting of that, we thirst no more. This is not sterile indifference to living. On the contrary, it realizes the Limitless Life to the full. To get rid of the will-to-live is not to lose interest in living. It is to put a plus sign for a minus.

We kill our bodies through our restless struggles to acquire what we already have. When life flows through us unobstructed, the balance of metabolism is maintained. Additionally, we enter into a different order of knowing. We discover ourselves and find that we were never born, nor shall we ever die. We learn that we are four-dimensional, not three-dimensional beings, and enter into a realm of power and joy without words.

The possessor of the twenty-fourth path is aware, and their subconsciousness weaves the realization into the very cells of their body. Externally they may appear to be like the rest of humanity. But they are a member of a new species.

They are God-taught. They know themselves, the eternal principles of their life, and perceive the celestial order surrounding them. Gone are all their old notions of safety and security. Their mouth speaks with a new tongue, and every word they utter is confirmed by outward manifestation.

Such individuals hold the balance of the world. We owe them all we know about justice, righteousness, and truth. Not from conquerors and worldly politicians does the progress of humanity come. It is from the simple seers that the race receives revelations. Read about their lives and words. All of them knew their essential immortality, and in that sublime, knowledge lost completely the thirst for life, which drives deluded souls to madness. Misinformed people dream of crossing the desert sands of "this world." However, the place where they suffer their nightmare torments is the Paradise of Glory and Peace.

The Eye of the Lord is everywhere, and when it opens in us, we shall share the Divine Vision.

CHAPTER 14

25th Path of Samekh

Experimental Intelligence

The 25th Path is the *Experimental or Testing Intelligence* (*Sekhel Nisyoni*). It is the primary test through which all the Merciful Ones become skilled.

הנתיב	חמשה	ו-עשרים	נקרא
Path	5	20	is called

שכל	נסיוני	מפני	שהוא
Intelligence	Experimental trial, test	because	It is

ה-נסיון	ה-קדמון	שבו	מנסה
the test	ancient,	through which	experience skilled, tested

ל-כל	ה-חסידים		
to all	Merciful Ones Saints		

The 25ᵗʰ Path is called the Tempting Intelligence because it is the primary temptation by which God tests pious people.

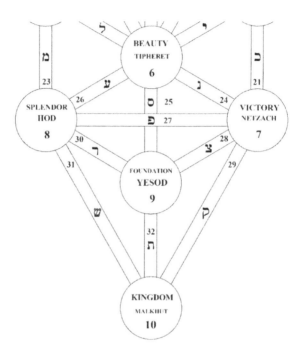

Experimental or Testing Intelligence

Nisyoni (נסיוני) means experimental. It is from the root, *nee.sahon* (נסיון) meaning, trial, test, experiment, experience. Nee.sahon is numerically equal to *yoh.az* (יועץ), meaning counselor and advisor.

"And he will be called Wonderful Counselor, Mighty God, Everlasting Father, Prince of Peace." – Isaiah 9:6.

Probation or Trial signifies testing the ideas and innovations the imagination suggests.

Samekh – ס

Numerically, Samekh is 60, the value of *bah.kan* (בחן) meaning, tried by fire, *examine, test, try, assay, prove, probe, purify,* and *check.* In Isaiah 28:16, "See, I lay a stone in Zion, a tested (בחן) stone (אבן), a precious cornerstone, a sure foundation; the one who believes will never be shaken."

Theoretical occult knowledge without test and trial is next to useless. Over the years, I've seen students believe that *since God is good and God made everything; therefore, all is good.* Then, they encounter a malevolent person, and their faith is shaken to the core. Remember what Master Jesus said, "Look, I am sending you out like sheep among wolves; therefore, be as shrewd as snakes and as innocent as doves." This is the test of the 25th Path of Experimental Intelligence.

Key 14, Temperance

Key 14, Temperance, is a pictorial representation of the test and trials of the path of Samekh. On the lion of Leo, the Archangel Michael pours the waters of Aquarius. Saturn rules Aquarius and suggests that passion must be tempered with discipline. On the right side is the Eagle of Scorpio, looking at the crown in the background. Its wings are outstretched and ready to take flight, symbolizing aspiration. Above his head are five fiery Yods (י) to symbolize that our lofty ambitions must be tempered by listening to the guidance from the silent voice (Key 5, the Hierophant) before taking flight. In Key 5, we receive instruction; in Key 14, the teachings are tested through experience.

231

The letter name Samekh (סמך) means *lean upon*, *support*, *uphold*. Our holy guardian angel tests us, sometimes to our limits. It wants us to rely upon it for support. And this is the "primary test through which all the Merciful Ones become skilled." The Merciful Ones are Chasidim (חסידים). It is from the root Chesed (הסד), the name of the fourth sephiroth.

Jupiter rules Sagittarius. Chesed is the Sphere of Jupiter, but what does that mean? From one perspective, a sephirah is a massive filing cabinet filled with ideas related to each other. Jupiter is a group of ideas that fit inside the Chesed filing cabinet. Therefore, Jupiter is a subset of Chesed.

Jupiter rules and is dignified by Triplicity by Night in Sagittarius. Jupiter is associated with faith. In Sagittarius, he is well dignified. One distinct characteristic of the Chasidim is their unshakable faith. They embody the Bible verse, "Cast your burden on the Lord, and he will sustain you." – Psalm 55:22

They seek to serve the One Self and align their will with God's Will. Therefore they depend entirely on Cosmic Life. The Chasidim faith sustains them through tests and trials. They do not weigh down responsibilities or dread taking action because it might create "bad karma." They know that the One Ego is the One Actor and has no fear and inspires no fear.

The Chasidim understand their feelings of personal ego come from the flow of energy coming into and flowing out of their personality. Therefore, their mental attitude is observing their daily life and constantly recalling that the One Ego performs their activities.

Regenerating Intelligence

The 26th Path is Regenerating Intelligence (Sekhel MeChudash). By it, the Blessed Holy One regenerates the whole World of Creation.

שכל	נקרא	ו-עשרים	ששה	ה-נתיב
Intelligence	is called	20	6	The Path

מחדש	ש"י ה	קב "ה	מפני	מחודש
Innovator	Blessed Holy One		because	renewed
rejuvenation				regenerate
Title of God				

ב-בריאת	ה-חדשים	כל	בו
in creation	renew,	all	By it
making	revive		
world			

קב "ה			ה-עולם
הוא	בריך	קודשא	the world
He (*Hu*)	Blessed be	The holy one	universe

ש "ה - שם המפרש - The Ineffable Name (God).

The 26th Path is called the Renewing Intelligence because, through it, all the things, which have been renewed during the world's creation, are renewed.

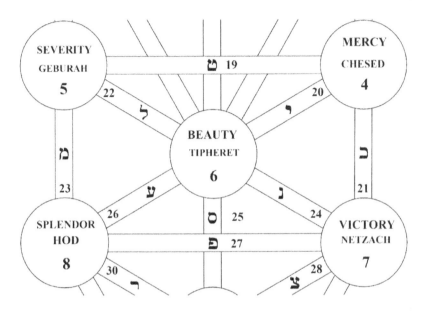

The 26th Path of wisdom carries the power of Ruach in Tiphareth down to Hod. It is the link between the Sphere of the Sun and the Sphere of Mercury, imagination and intellect, and between the Egoic Body and the Mental Body. This path has to do with the means whereby the EGO in Tiphareth effects changes in our personal intellect, which corresponds to Hod at the lower end of the Path of Ayin.

Ayin - ע

Numerically, Ayin is 70, the number of years of a human in the Bible. Seventy is also the number of days that the star Sirius is below the horizon before its annual heliacal rising and the number of years that the Jews were in captivity in Babylon. The number seventy is a numerical symbol of bondage before a new beginning.

The path of Ayin is the continuation of the twentieth path (Yod, The Hermit). Both paths are connected with mental and physical vision.

Key 15, The Devil

Key 15, The Devil, is associated with Bondage. Bondage brings misery and ignorance. But our suffering motivates us to change our lives and circumstances. The means to release us from sorrow is shown on the belly of the beast - Mercury. We must look into the environment instead of relying on surface appearances.

The Number 15 is the extension of 5 (1 + 2 + 3 + 4 + 5 = 15). Five is the number of The Hierophant. Pain and suffering are the universal language and the ultimate teacher. The composition of Key 15 includes certain resemblances to that of Key 5, together with equally emphatic differences.

Letter Name Ayin - עין

The letter name Ayin (עין) means *eye* and the sense of sight and the expression of knowledge, character, etc. *Ayin* also means *spring* or *fountain*. The eye is one of four bodily "fountains," the other three being the mouth, skin, and urethra. Sweat releases excessive heat from the body, urine evacuates toxins, and the eye produces water during grief or pain. All have to do with cleansing.

Life-power is the Creator, Preserver, and Destroyer (Renovator). During change, old things pass away. Humanity clings to the familiar and distrusts change. Letting go of our theories and conceptions concerning people and circumstances is painful. The same areas that register physical pain are activated in our brains when we encounter new ideas contrary to our cherished ideals.

Capricorn - ♑

In the Sepher Yetzirah, Ayin is attributed to Capricorn. Saturn rules Capricorn. However, Mars is dignified by Exaltation and Triplicity. In Capricorn, Mars is more dignified than Saturn.

You can see the Mars aggression in others when you challenge the mainstream narrative with logic and reason. How dare you provide information that challenges their beliefs.

You can only lift yourself out of bondage and, perhaps, by your example, help others. But if you challenge people's beliefs directly, expect a fight.

That is why seventy is the number of Ayin, and *he.sha* (הסה) to be silent.

MeChudash (מחודש) means Renewing or Renovating, and its numeral value, 358, is the same as the numeration of Nachash (נחש) and Messiah (משיח). Nachash is the serpent of temptation in Genesis. The same word is used for copper in the book of Daniel. Copper is the metal of Venus and is a symbol of our desire nature. Messiah (the anointed) is the redeemer that leads us from temptation.

Recall the story of the prodigal son in Luke 15:11-32.

The Prodigal Son leaves his father's house and follows his desires (Venus) into the densest matter. When his money runs out, his friends leave him. Poor and needy, he eats the husks or shells (*klipoth*, קליפות) that were rejected by pigs. Then the son (בן) returns to his father (אב) the perfected stone (אבן).

Thus, in the first half of the cycle, Venus is the seducer that leads to humanity's fall. However, we still feel something is missing once we have fulfilled our desires. The small still voice of the One Ego influences us unconsciously until we awaken. Then we actively listen to the Voice and participate consciously in our evolution.

Winston Churchill said, "You can always count on the Americans to do the right thing after they have tried everything else." Unfortunately, this is true for all humanity. I find my mistakes are far more instructive than my successes. Through successive struggles and failures, we grow wise and see things through different eyes, and the world is made new.

CHAPTER 15

27th Path of Peh

The 27th Path is the Perceptible or Felt Intelligence (Sekhel Murgash). Through it, the senses of all living beings under the zodiac are excited.

נקרא	ו-עשרים	שבעה	ה-נתיב
is called	20	7	The Path

חומר	ו-הוא	מורגש	שכל
material	& it	felt, perceived perceptible	Intelligence

ה-נבראים	נבראו	שממנו	מפני
living creature(s)	were created his creatures humanity	from which through	because

ה-עליון	גלגל	מתחת	כל
high, exalted The Most High Title of God	revolve zodiac	below, under beneath	all

רגש	ו-ה-רגשותם
To be excited, to rage Emotion, sense	and the feelings

239

The 27th Path is called Provocative Intelligence, and it is the matter from which all the things produced under the Supreme Sphere have been created and their movements.

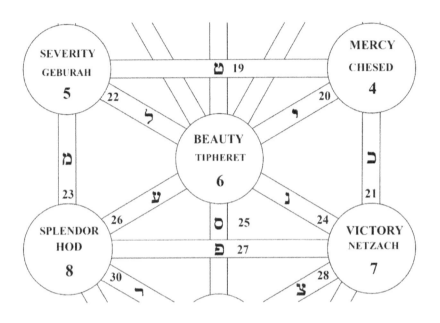

Peh is the reciprocal Path that joins Hod and Netzach. Mars – harmony through conflict joins the seat of Intellect and Desire. It is Provocative Intelligence, and it follows Renewing Intelligence because the sense of limitation sooner or later gives way to the conviction that this limitation is not permanent. This conviction is man's chief incentive to the activities leading to freedom. This conviction is an intuitive perception that the Spirit of man is one with the Universal Spirit, which, as we have seen, must necessarily succeed in carrying out the great purpose for which it projects Itself in a universe.

Peh – פ

Peh is numerically 80. As a pictograph, Peh is a mouth with a tongue. On the Tree, the paths of Daleth (Venus) and Peh (Mars) are like nature because they are both horizontal paths. However, they are opposite in appearance. Peh is the central letter and the heart of Nephesh (נפש), the vital soul seated in Yesod. Peh is also numerically equal to Yesod (יסוד), Foundation. And Yesod can be rewritten as Sod Yod (סוד י), the secret of Yod. And this secret is the life force, Chaiah (י), which energizes Peh.

Key 16, The Tower

Key 16, the Tower, symbolizes the second stage of spiritual unfoldment – awakening. Place Key 16, The Tower, horizontally on the Tree of Life along the path of Peh. The crown's tower is near Hod, and the base is at Netzach. The Sun in the upper right-hand corner is next to Tiphareth. It is the One Ego in Tiphareth that awakens us so that we can free ourselves from bondage. (Interestingly, the BOTA version of the TOL has Key 16 with the base near Hod and the tower near Netzach.)

Peh (פה) means mouth and is synonymous with speech as an organ of expression. The letter name Peh is 85, and this is the value of *Boaz* (בועז), the black pillar of severity set before Solomon's temple and *ha.mam* (הםם) meaning, to frighten, confound, stun and confuse.

Words are used to inspire courage or fear in Proverbs 15:1, 2, and 4. "A gentle answer deflects anger, but harsh words make tempers flare. The tongue of the wise commends knowledge, but the mouths of fools pour out folly. The soothing tongue is a Tree of Life, but a perverse tongue crushes the spirit."

Mars - ♂

The first stage of spiritual unfoldment is fear, ignorance, and misery. The only way we overcome bondage is by facing our problems boldly. Mars represents the willpower or volition to overcome obstacles.

Murgash (מורגש) means perceptible. The adjective is from the root ra.gash (רגש), meaning roar, rage, and upheaval. These meanings relate to the Mars-force attributed to Key 16 and Peh. The Mars force is exciting and active in reproduction. It is a manifestation of the Holy Influence, Mezla, flowing through the Tree of Life and represented by the lightning flash in Key 16. Perceptible Intelligence is so intense that it is tangible. Anyone in a crowd with their passions stirred can experience Perceptible Intelligence.

Magical Power of Peh

The magical power attributed to the 27th Path is "To foresee all future events that do not depend on a superior free will or an all undiscernible cause." The choice of words here is subtle. No event depends on any personal "superior free will" because all events depend on the One Will, which finds expression through every living creature. It is what excites every creature into action and constitutes its essential life.

The 28th Path is called Natural Intelligence (Sekhel Mutba). This is because it completes and perfects the nature of all that exists under the revolution of the Sun.

נקרא	ו-עשרים	שמנה	ה-נתיב
is called	& 20	8	The Path

שבו	מפני	מוטבע	שכל
It is	Because	Innate, Inborn	Intelligence
		natural	

ה-נמצים	כל	טבע	נשלם
existing	all	nature	completed
		character	

ב-שלימות	ה-חמה	גלגל	מתחת
perfected	The Sun	revolve	under
complete		circuit of the sun	below

244

The 28th Path is called Natural Intelligence because, through it, the nature of every existing thing under the orbit of the Sun has been completely perfected.

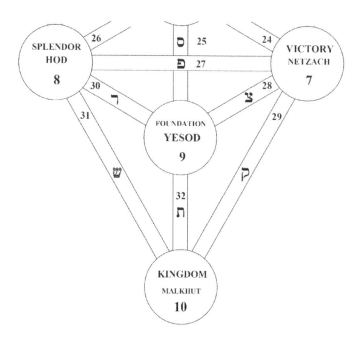

Tzaddi - צ

Tzaddi is numerically 90, and so is Mem (מים), meaning water. Tzaddi means side. Specifically, a man lying on his side and waiting for prey. Nun (נ), the Imaginative Intelligence, gives form to the imaginations of all Living Creatures. To imagine new ideas, we must still have the watery mind stuff. In Hebrew, *silence* is *du.mahm* (דומם) and is also numbered 90.

Key 17, The Star

The woman in Key 17, The Star, kneels in a pool of water. Her legs form the shape of the Tav (ת). Place Key 17 on the path between Netzach and Yesod on the Tree of Life. Notice the pool is Yesod.

The bird on the tree is an ibis, a fishing bird and a hunter. What we desire, we focus our attention on. The ibis is sacred to Thoth, who is associated with Mercury. Notice that Hod, the sphere of Mercury, is on the same side of the Tree of Life as the Ibis bird.

You were taught the Tarot lessons' central yellow star stands for the Quintessence (Fifth Essence). The eight-spoked wheel on the Fool's dress, the Wheel of Fortune, and the great star symbolize the Life-power setting the world in motion. Chaiah streams from Chokmah down the right-hand pillar of Mildness through the Hierophant paths and The Wheel of Fortune into Netzach. In Netzach, the life-force manifests as our desires of what the Primal Will to Good has already prepared for us.

Note also that Jakin (יכין), the Pillar of Mildness or righthand pillar in King Solomon's Temple, is numerically 90, the number of Tzaddi printed on Key 17.

Letter Name Tzaddi - צדי

Tzaddi (צדי) means a man lying on his side. Spelled *tza.dah* (צדה), it means to lie in wait, ambush, lurk, and scheme. This symbolizes the means of investigating the unseen. Research into the depths of inner consciousness, represented by water. Such hunting for inner knowledge is the function of meditation.

246

Aquarius - ♒

Saturn rules Aquarius and is the principle of limitation. Therefore, meditation requires the restriction of our thoughts around a central idea.

Uranus also rules Aquarius. In Greek mythology, Urania was one of the Muses, specifically the goddess of astronomy. The muses are a personified force of inspiration for a creative artist. In Aquarius, Uranus, the spirit of originality, and Saturn, the lord of discipline, are dignified.

Natural Intelligence

Mutba (מוטבע) means natural. It is derived from the root *tah.vah* (טבע), meaning, *to sink, drown, coin, impress*, and *stamp*. With different pointing, the same letters spell teh.bah, meaning nature, character, element, and substance.

These definitions suggest that nature is like the impression made on wax by a signet ring. The element Water takes an impression formed by our thoughts. After it manifests, it completes and perfects its nature under the revolution of the Sun.

CHAPTER 16

29th Path of Qoph - ק

Physical Intelligence

The 29th Path is *Physical Intelligence* (Sekhel Mugsham). It depicts and establishes the growth of all physical bodies incorporated under the Zodiac.

הנתיב	תשעה	ו-עשרים	נקרא
Path	9	& 20	is called

שכל	מוגשם	מפני	שהוא
Intelligence	physical corporal	because	It is

מתאר	כל	גשם	שית-גשם
Described Depicted	All every	physical body	incorporated

תחת	תכונת	ה-גלגלים	ב-גידולים
Under	established	the revolutions the zodiac	growth

The 29th Path is called Corporal Intelligence because it molds each body, which is materialized under the organization of all the Spheres and their increments.

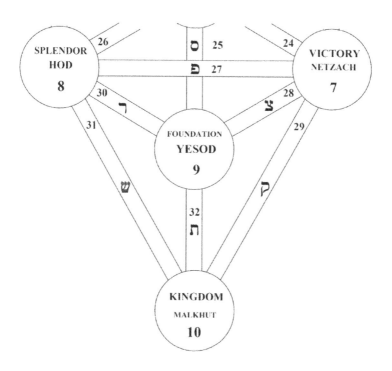

Letter Name Qoph קוֹף

Qoph (קוֹף) means monkey or ape. The same letters form *kuf* meaning a needle's eye, a hole (for an ax). From the same root is *ha.kafah* (הקפה), meaning *circling, encirclement, circuit,* and *round.*

Mugsham (מוגשם) is from the verb *gahsham* (גשם), meaning *substance, matter, rain* or a *hard rain shower*. The Key 18 symbolism includes a shower of eighteen Yods (י). Their number, 18, is numerically *chai* (חי), life. Because they are Yods, the total is 18 x 10, or 180. This is the number of degrees in a semicircle. The sun follows the path of a semicircle from east to west during the day. Therefore, 180 (degrees) is a symbol of the day or incarnation period of a personality.

The same word is pronounced *gee.shem* means *to carry out, realize, effect,* and *execute*.

The Holy Guardian Angel manages the process of embodiment. Even during gestation, the fetus's development is under the One Ego's direction, which takes full possession of that body when the child draws its first breath. The One Ego is present through growth and adulthood until the One Ego withdraws its sustaining presence at the moment of death.
The conscious and subconscious activities of the personal vehicle are continuously under the guidance of the indwelling One Ego, symbolized as the angel of Key 14.

Key 18, The Moon

Placing Key 18 along the twenty-ninth path, the Moon is near Netzach, and the pool is by Malkuth. The 18-rayed moon emits eighteen Yods, the number of chai (חי) meaning *living, alive, vivacious, active, fresh, strong,* and *healthy*. The root word of Chaiah (חיה) is the life-force stream from Chokmah down the Pillar of Mildness to Netzach.

The 4th Stage of Spiritual Unfoldment – Organization

When a human arrives at the Great Work stage, where they begin to meditate, they think they're struggling upward along the path in Key 18. They have ups and downs. Often they are in the dark, but as they draw nearer the goal, they enjoy periods of enlightenment. They wax and wane like the light of the moon, and there are periods of darkness between them. During dark nights, only the light of the stars shows the path. This is when the physiological changes resulting from meditation are built into the structure of the human body. This is the fourth stage of spiritual unfoldment assigned to Qoph – Organization.

As a consequence of these changes, old brain cells are gradually eliminated. New brain cells embody new ideas. Then one realizes that personality is the vehicle, or instrument, of the One Ego. The Ego is in perfect union with the universal life-force (Ab, the Father) and the Divine Soul, Neshamah. Ab, the Father, is the life-force of Yekhidah, the One Self. Aima, the Mother, is the Divine Soul proceeding from that same Yekhidah. Ben, the Son, is the One Ego in Tiphareth, the Holy Angel directing the Great Work of liberation.

The completion of the Great Work is symbolized in Key 20. It is the "resurrection of the body." The activity of the twenty-ninth path is involved in it. Without the reorganization, the physical vehicle is not raised from the "death" of three-dimensional consciousness into "eternal life." It is the adept's conscious awareness that they were never born and will never die. With this awareness goes first-hand knowledge that one is and has always been a four-dimensional being. The adept exercises powers that are present in every human personality. Illumination allows the adept at knowing them; through this knowledge, they develop skills in their exercise.

The main work of Corporeal Intelligence is making bodies peculiar to the twelve zodiac signs. The text says of Corporeal Intelligence, "It depicts and establishes the growth of all physical bodies incorporated under the Zodiac." Illumination is not a loss of personal identity. It does not erase the characteristics which make the Taurus distinguishable from a Libra. Thus, the Holy City symbol in the Apocalypse has twelve gates and twelve foundations, and the seer's vision makes it evident that these are the zodiacal types. Illumination does not erase personality. It enlightens and liberates. Adepts do not lose their identity.

Nothing is added. Yet, the sign of liberation is a *plus*, not a *minus*. Personality remains distinct, but the bondage of the delusion of separateness is overcome. One share the upward vision of Spirit.

One sees oneself as linked eternally to the White Brilliance of the Crown. Just as a light ray is continuous with the sun whence it goes forth, so is the ray of Spirit at the center of every personality, continuous with the ONE LIGHT and ONE LIFE of the Cosmic Self.

Western Meditation Techniques

Meditation has always been associated with breath control. The Western School recommends the establishment of rhythmic, deep breathing as the partly conscious and partly subconscious function of the lungs. Western methods of training pay more attention to emotional and intellectual processes because it has been found that breathing may be made rhythmic and regular by practices that are directed primarily to mind control. Western practice considers that direct concentration on any bodily center or function may result in congestion of the organs involved in that function.

Consequently, it is safer to concentrate on symbols or activities that necessitate these centers' functioning. Among the best symbols for this purpose is the Tarot. For example, instead of direct concentration on the Moon center, one uses the picture of the High Priestess. Far better than focusing on the center at the spine's base is a meditation on Key 21.

Besides the Tarot, colors and musical notes are related to chakras. The divine names corresponding to the Sephiroth from Binah to Yesod inclusive may be employed to rouse the planetary centers' activity. They should be intoned on a monotone or use the musical notes associated with the planetary force. They also can be sung, with the proper note for each letter. The latter practice is more difficult, and beginners should use a single tone. For example, Elohim (pronounced *ale.oh.heem*, with the accent on the last syllable) is intoned to the note A for the center at the base of the spine.

This last method is safe. However, it may be made even more effective using an equilateral triangle, point downward, and tinted deep indigo (or blue-violet) to correlate the color with the sound. This particular triangle is recommended because the down-pointing equilateral is a symbol for water and is also one of the correspondences to 3 and Binah, the third Sephirah.

There are more complicated combinations of geometrical figures, colors, and sounds. Instruction concerning these is not suitable for this elementary lesson. However, alert students will have little difficulty working out the colors, tones, and geometrical forms appropriate for the Sephiroth from Binah to Yesod, A polygon having sides corresponding to the Sephirah number or a star having the same amount of rays as the Sephirah may be drawn and colored to use in this practice until one can visualize it. After some training, both color and intonation can be imagined clearly.

If you cannot determine the correct pitch, use the geometrical figure. Look steadily at it for about two minutes. Then make your intonation without any attempt to strike the right tone. We have found that the monotone, which comes spontaneously, is rarely in dissonance with the correct sound corresponding to the color. It may not be the exact tone, but it will nearly always be in harmony with it – which means that it will be one of the harmonic overtones of that particular note. No harm has followed in the few instances that a note is sung, dissonant with the color. If one practices faithfully, the tone chanted will correspond to the color. Even with persons without a musical ear, this technique is effective.

The divine names corresponding to the seven planetary Sephiroth are given in Appendix 6. They are the colors of the Sephiroth in Briah, the creative world. No others should be used for this practice.

Magical Power of Qoph

Eliphas Levi's manuscript says the magical power of a possessor of the path of Qoph is "To triumph over adversities." This is a concise summary of the embodiment process, which is the work of Physical Intelligence. The changes in our organisms are brought about by struggles to overcome adverse conditions. The changes from natural humanity to the new creature directly result from our attempts to climb out of our troubles.

Collective Intelligence

The 30th Path is called Collective or Inclusive Intelligence (Sekhel Kelali). Through it, astrologers study the laws governing the stars and zodiac and perfect their knowledge.

נתיב	שלשים	נקרא	שכֹל
Path	30	is called	Intelligence

כללי	מפני	כוללים	הוברי
Collective	because of	comprehensive	Astrologers
Universal		inclusive	

שמים	ב-משפטיהם	ה-ככבים	וה-מזלות
Heavens	Justice	to shine	*Mazloth*
	Laws	(stars)	Zodiac

עיונם	תשלומי	ידיעתם	ב-אופני
theoretical	completion	*Da'ath*	Ophan
speculative	payment	knowledge	wheels

גלגלים			
wheels			
to revolve			

The 30th Path is called Deductive Intelligence because Astrologers deduct their speculations from it by evaluating the stars and celestial signs. They derive the perfection of their knowledge from observing their revolving motions.

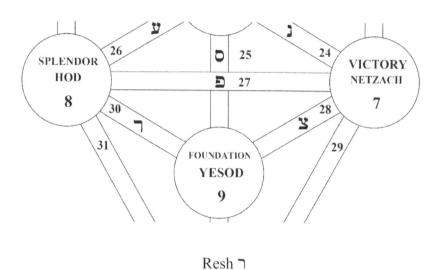

Resh ר

Resh is 200, which is the value of *eh.tzem* (עצם), meaning *bone, object, substance, essence*. Pronounced *oh.tzem,* it means *strength, might,* and *force.* This word is used throughout the Thirty-two Paths of wisdom and translated as "essence."

Collective *kelali* (כללי) is from the root *kol* (כלל), signifying *all, whole,* and *complete.* The thirtieth path participates in the completion of the Great Work. The personality is the instrument or vehicle through which the Life-power evolves the new creature. The angel in Key 14 symbolizes the active transforming power of the Holy Guardian Angel. The One Ego, the Christos, is personified by Horus, Krishna, Brother R. C., and Freemasonry as Hiram Abiff.

This evolution is brought about by the cosmic life-force, Chaiah, seated in Chokmah. This power is universal radiant energy. Consequently, it is associated with the stars and the zodiac.

Adepts

An adept can be of any race. Perhaps their eyes and facial expression will be the most prominent points of external difference. Their behavior and speech are different than their contemporaries. They do what seems to be impossible for ordinary men and women. They have unusual insight and can "conquer love and hate," for they will command devotion from their disciples and overcome enemies' antagonism. They are free from attachment to people and things, and the "pairs of opposites" will not disturb their calm poise.

Adepts are chemically and structurally different from ordinary humans. There are other constituents in their bloodstream. Currents of nervous force pass in their organism through open channels closed in ordinary men's and women's bodies. Centers in the nervous system, brain, and corresponding glands function differently.

Consequently, an adept's ideas of their world differ widely from ordinary conceptions. Moreover, they have different ''receptors" from those of natural humanity. Consequently, they interpret the universe and their environment differently.

Their different organism gives adepts a different vision. The main difference is that they know how to solve problems and have the necessary successes to give them confidence. They approach their difficulties with joy. But there is plenty for them to do and learn.

Adepts are *baali ha-shamem* (בעלי השמים), masters of the heavens. Please do not confuse them with ordinary astrologers. Besides knowing and interpreting the external celestial forces' influences, they are masters of their *interior* stars. This mastery is a consequence of the meditation symbolized in Tarot by Key 17.

Key 19 is a picture of something which occurs at both conscious and subconscious levels. The Path of Resh represents the early stages of our conscious awareness that we are becoming a new creatures.

Notice in Key 19 that the boy is on the side corresponding to Hod and the girl on the side of Netzach. The Sun is near Hod, and the fairy ring is by Yesod. The orange Yods are grouped in a pattern 6-1-6. This is the number of Yom (יום) with the final Mem (ם) equal to 600. Yom means day or a period of incarnation or manifestation. With different pointing, it means *warm* and *bright*.

There are 125 lines at are around the sun's face. 125 is 5^3 or 5 x 5 x 5. This is the three-fold manifestation of Geburah or Law. Note that the 30th Path of Resh begins on the left-hand Pillar of Severity.

The children in Key 19 stand with one foot in the inner circle of the fairy ring. This stage of unfoldment is a preliminary to the two that come after it.

Although the thirtieth path does connect with the completion of the Great Work, it represents the youth rather than the maturity of the liberated personality. Here we have something comparable to the completion of an airplane.

It rolls off the assembly line and out to the field, where it will first be tested and then sent to the various missions of war and peace. The work of making it is ended. Its work is just beginning. This is indicated by Key 19, which shows 9, the number of completion, as the active principle working through 1, a numeral symbol of the beginning. What follows is discussed in the next chapter.

CHAPTER 17

31st Path of Shin - שׁ

Perpetual Intelligence

The 31st Path is *Perpetual Intelligence* (Sekhel Tamidi). It regulates all the cyclic forces that form the revolutions of the zodiac (masloth).

ה-נתיב	אחד	ו-שלשים	נקרא
The Path	1	and 30	is called

שכל	תמידי	מפני	שהוא
Intelligence	continuous	Because of	It is
	consistent		
	perpetual		

כלל	כחות	כל	ה-גלגלים
rule	Power(s)	all	to cause
regulates	Forces		to revolve

ו-מזלות	ו-ה-צורות	ו-משפטיהם	
Mazloth	& the form(s)	and Law	
zodiac	shapes	theorem	
		their judgments	

The 31st Path is called Deductive Intelligence because it also comprehends all the effects of the Spheres, the celestial signs, their forms (or images), and their configuration and evaluation.

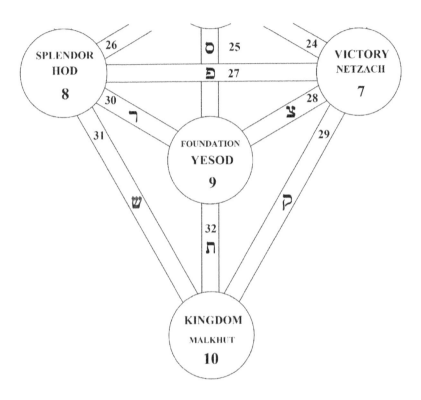

"The secret of the shin is the flame [Divine Revelation] bound to the coal (Divine Essence).

"One of the meanings of the word *shin* (שין) is *she.nu* (שינוי), change. The coal symbolizes the changeless essence, the secret of the verse: I am G-d, I have not changed,' meaning that relative to G-d's Essence, absolute no change has occurred before Creation to after Creation. The inner flame is the paradoxically latent presence of the power of change within the changeless." – *The Hebrew Letters*, p. 310.

Tamidi (תמידי) is from the root *tah.meed* (תמיד), signifying continuance, or indefinite extension, and perpetual time.

Note the last word of the text is *mishpatiham* (משפטיהם), "their judgments." The "revolutions of the zodiacs" are the cycles of successive incarnations. The form of their judgments is a veiled reference to the completion of the incarnation cycle by the "resurrection" from what St. Paul calls "the body of this death" (Romans 7:24). This is the "natural body," the body of sin, dominated by the vital soul and not yet perfected by the EGO.

Yet this "body of death" or "natural body" is the seed of the spiritual body, which finally evolved after the creative process. What raises it from corruption is the spiritual fire that enters it through the channel of the 31st Path.

Perpetual Intelligence is the spiritual power that, without a single break in the continuity of its operation, works to perfect every one of its personal vehicles by providing each of them with the new creature's spiritual body. Perpetual Intelligence is even now at work within you. It is even now preparing you for the event pictured by the symbols of Key 20.

Complementary Paths Qoph and Shin

The Path of Qoph is chiefly concerned with the corporeal pattern and form. It carries our desire nature into the sphere of physical sensation. Its opposite, the 31st Path of Shin, carries into the physical organism the influences descending from Kether through the side of Geburah on the Tree. The whole series of paths on the pillar of severity has to do with activities which, from the ordinary human standpoint, are concerned with the future, with the elaboration of the consequences of what the One Self knows itself to be into forms of expression which make that knowledge manifest in actual states of realization.

For this reason, Key 20, corresponding to the 31st Path, is a symbol of a state of human personality, which is the "future" for most human beings.

Supernal Triad

From the 24th to the 32^{nd,} paths are powers working in the field of personality. The Qabalistic constitution of humanity includes three divisions.

The Divine Triad, Kether, Chokmah, and Binah are the highest and innermost. These correspond to the cosmic One Self, Yekhidah, Chaiah, the life-force, and Neshamah, the Divine Soul.

Egoic Triad

The triad of Individuality or Egoic Triad is a mediator between it and the outer and lowest triad. The Egoic Triad members are Chesed, Geburah, and Tiphareth, or memory, volition, and imagination focused in the One Ego seated in the sixth Sephirah. The One Ego is the reflection of Yekhidah in Kether.

Under the control of the One Ego, personality is evolved. Our characters pass from the astral plane into embodiment through birth. At death, the One Ego withdraws its coordinating and cohesive influence from the physical plane. Still, it continues to exert this influence on the astral vehicle until the time comes for another incarnation.

Here the Western School's doctrine is at variance with Theosophical opinions, which say that in due course, the astral vehicle is left by the One Ego to disintegrate. Instead, the Western School says this occurs infrequently. Only when a prolonged period of evil action severely injures the astral vehicle does the One Ego abandon the astral body. Then it waits for an opportunity to send forth the finer personal vehicles (desire-body and mental body) in combination with a newly formed astral organism. When this occurs, it is what is meant by the New Testament teaching on the "second death."

Even such an apparent failure is not final. The One Ego permits the astral vehicle to disintegrate, but this does not end life. Instead, it is temporarily "out of circulation." The individual is like one with a severe illness, must miss a year of school, and loses touch with their former classmates.

Understanding why such apparent failures occur is difficult, but setbacks of this kind do happen. The One Ego, though identical to the Christos, is not the all-perfect One Self. Thus "The Father and I are in union" is a better translation of Jesus' declaration than "The Father and I are one." Nevertheless, there is never a total failure. The unique tendency of the Life-power ultimately finds adequate manifestation. Rest assured that the destiny of every human being is the perfect fulfillment of this unique tendency.

Lower Mind Triad

Below the Egoic Triad is the triad of the lower mind, comprising Netzach (desire nature), Hod (intellect), and Yesod (vital soul). These powers descend into the sphere of sensation and physical embodiment through the paths of Qoph (ק), Shin (ש), and Tav (ת).

The path of Qoph carries the powers of the desire nature into the physical body. Shin carries the energies of intellect. Tav's path links the vital soul (Yesod) and its physical instrument (Malkuth).

Thus Qoph's path is chiefly concerned with the physical pattern and form. Its opposite, the thirty-first path of Shin (ש), carries into the physical organism the influences descending from Kether through the side of Geburah on the Tree. It begins with the twelfth path, which brings the Holy Influence from Kether to Binah. It continues through the eighteenth path to Geburah, then descending through the twenty-third path to Hod and completing the line of descent employing the thirty-first path from Hod to Malkuth.

The paths on the Geburah side of the Tree are activities concerned with the future. It symbolizes the elaboration of the consequences of what the One Self knows itself to be into forms of expression that manifest that knowledge in actual states of realization.

Key 20, corresponding to the thirty-first path, symbolizes a state of human personality, the "future" for most human beings. Not for all. Some have advanced beyond it to more exalted spiritual unfoldment.

Western School does not teach a way to escape incarnation. On the contrary, it holds that the Great Work aims at perfected embodiment – "Thy kingdom come, thy will be done, on earth as it is in heaven."

The cycles of the zodiac are successive incarnations. Their judgment (מששפטיהם) is a veiled reference to the completion of the incarnation cycle by the resurrection from "the body of this death" (Romans 7:24). This is the natural body dominated by the vital soul and not yet perfected by the One Ego.

Yet, the natural body is the seed of the spiritual body, which finally evolved after the creative process. What raises it from corruption is the spiritual fire that enters it through the channel of the thirty-first path.

The angel in Key 20 is Gabriel, whose name is from the same root as Geburah. Gabriel is the Divine Presence manifested as the overwhelming strength of volition. He is the sounder of the last trumpet, and Key 20 shows that sound is active, raising the new creature.

The One Ego is the angel here, just like the one in Key 14. Gabriel is the angel of Water and the western quarter of the heavens. Thus he is the angel of completion. The Seven Spirits are aspects of

ONE BEING. The ONE appears as Gabriel (West, Water), Raphael (East, Air)), Michael (South, Fire), and Uriel (North, Earth).

Seven rays extend from the angel's trumpet to show that the seven Elohim powers are combined in the sound, bringing the resurrected figures from their floating stone coffins.

Until this final consummation of the Great Work, we seem to be directing it from the intellectual, self-conscious awareness field. We make plans. We concentrate, study, and practice, Yet the final liberation is a call from above. It is not our work but the operation of the fiery Spirit.

Perpetual Intelligence is the spiritual power that works to perfect every one of its vehicles by providing each of them with the new creature's spiritual body. This body is incarnate on the physical plane, but it is freed from the necessity for birth and death. It begins its final incarnation as a natural body but ends that incarnation transmuted into the liberated adept immortal vehicle.

When this occurs, the physical vehicle can be "laid down" and taken up again. So men and women walk the earth today in bodies they have kept intact and youthful for centuries. Sometimes they lay them down voluntarily. Often to avoid curiosity by surviving their contemporaries.

Perpetual Intelligence is even now at work within you. It is now preparing you for the event pictured by Key 20. Perhaps that event may seem to you to be far in the future, but you will profit by remembering that both "past" and "future" are terms belonging to our natural time sense. They are meaningless to a human being who has risen from the grave of error into the light of knowledge.

270

This is the Great Work's inevitable fruition, whereby the One Ego brings its vehicles to completion as new creatures.

Serving Intelligence

The 32nd Path is Serving Intelligence (Sekhel Ne'evad). It repairs (Tikkun) all the operations of the seven planets and keeps them in their orbits.

נקרא	ו-שלשים	שנים	נתיב
is called	& 30	2	Path

שחוא	מפני	נעבד	שכל
It is	because	work	Intelligence
		serving	

ב-עבודת	תמשים	לכל	מתוקן
work(s)	realize	To all	repairs
operations			

ל-חבלם	לכת	כככי	שבעה
to orbit	to go	planets	7
orbiting		stars	

272

The 32nd Path is called the Aiding Intelligence because it quickly points toward all the seven planets' operations and their parts.

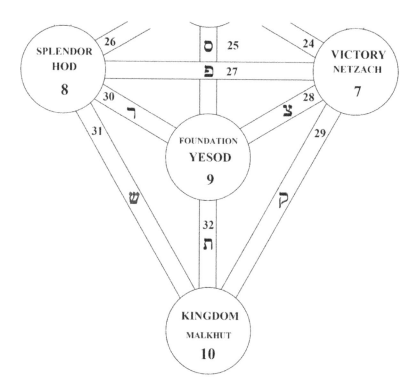

Tav is the only path proceeding from Yesod, joining the Sphere of the Moon, to the Sphere of the Elements, the field of the automatic consciousness and the vital soul, to the field of sensation and physical embodiment. Without the propagative power of Yesod, the Resplendent Intelligence of Malkuth would be barren and unproductive.

Tav - ת

"The tav, the final letter of the alef-beit, corresponds to Malchut (kingdom), the final Divine power, in the secret of "your Kingdom is the Kingdom of all worlds." The impression of the tav is the secret of the power that links worlds – generations – together." – *The Hebrew Letters*, p. 324

Serving Intelligence

Ne'evad (נעבד) is from the root *eh.ved* (עבד), meaning *enslaved person, bondsman, servant, servitor,* and *worshipper (of God)*. "The greatest among you shall be your servant." – Matthew 23:11

Letter Name Tav - תו

The letter-name Tav (תו) signifies a mark or signature. Therefore, Ezekiel implies its meaning is salvation because it was a mark set on the foreheads of those who were to be saved from death (Ezekiel 9:4).

As a number, the letter-name Tav (תו) is 406. It is the second extension from 7. The theosophic extension of 7 is 28. Therefore, the extension of 28 is 406 (the sum of the numbers from 0 to 28). Hence, Tav fully develops what Zain symbolizes (ז, 7) and the seventeenth path of wisdom.

A signature is a distinctive mark that validates a legal document. It is a mark of identification. Signatures are used daily to distinguish between personalities.

Thus Tav partakes in the quality of discrimination associated with Zain, the Disposing Intelligence.

These clues suggest the thirty-second path is related to the seventeenth path. Zain's path conducts Holy Influence from Binah (Sphere of Saturn) down to Tiphareth (Sphere of the Sun) and the One Ego seat. In the *Sefer Yetzirah*, Zain is assigned to Gemini, where Saturn is dignified by Triplicity. Using the astrology key, we see the link between Saturn (21st Path) and Gemini (17th Path).

Mercury rules Gemini, pictured as the Magician, Key 1. The psychological activity of concentration, leading to specialization, is what the Magician symbolizes. Restrictive activity is assigned to Saturn.

Right discrimination is pictured by Key 6. It uses this same Saturn quality to distinguish between conscious and subconscious functions necessary to establish balance. Remember that "above" and "within" are synonyms in western mysteries. Consequently, the mountain peak in the background of Key 6, and the angel to whom the woman lifts her eyes, are both symbols of the central Spiritual Presence. Union with that Presence is the goal of spiritual attainment. The mountain top is comparable to the single point at the pyramid's apex – the CENTRAL POINT.

In the Cube of Space, the CENTRAL POINT is innermost. This is the "Palace of Holiness in the midst," the Holy Temple at the center. The *Book of Formation* says the temple or palace corresponds to Tav. The other double letters correspond to the directions Above and Below and the four cardinal points. They are related to the planets and the faces of the cube.

Letter	Planet	Direction
Beth	Mercury	Above
Gimel	The Moon	Below
Daleth	Venus	East
Kaph	Jupiter	West
Peh	Mars	North
Resh	The Sun	South
Tav	Saturn	Center

Tikkun תקון

The text says the Path of Tav "repairs all the operations of the
seven planets and keeps them in their orbits."
Tikkun means to repair, specifically repair after the Shattering of
the Vessels. In the Qabalah, before this universe, was another.
First, the sephiroth existed as a unity, then they divided. In this
primitive state, the sephiroth are called "vessels." They were
vessels of God's light but unable to interact with each other.
Therefore, they couldn't hold the divine light and shattered. This is
called the "Breaking of the Vessels."

Then God rectified (tikkun) the vessels, and they could interact
with each other, and the sephiroth could give and receive. God
repairs all the worlds, but this one.

If God were to reveal himself in the physical plane fully, it would
cease to exist. Therefore, from one perspective, God created
humanity to repair the physical plane. This is called *tikkun olam*
(תקון עולם), "repair of the world."

Hence our text says that Administrative Intelligence "repairs all the seven planets' operations and keeps them in their orbits." The central presence is symbolized in the Apocalypse by the Lamb. The Lamb is the light of the city. The Lamb, in union with the Lord God Almighty, constitutes the inner temple of the city. The throne of God and the Lamb are amid this crystalline, golden cube, and the river of living water flows from the throne, clear as crystal.

Forget all your early religious training and prejudices. Consider the symbols carefully. You cannot miss their true meaning, for they were taken from the Seer of Patmos, the same treasure-house of images you possess and yours to use and understand.

The Holy City is also called the Bride, a title of Malkuth, the tenth Sephirah. She is the world-dancer of Key 21. Her name, Kallah (כלה), is usually translated *bride* or *spouse*, and *crowned one*, and is from the root *kallal* (כלל), "complete, perfect." The Greek for *bride* is *nymphe* (νυμφη), which in Greek gematria is 998, the number of *Kore Kosmou*, "Virgin of the World." In a Greco-Egyptian occult book ascribed to Hermes, the Virgin of the World refers to Isis-Sophia, the Virgin Bride. She is the revealer of instruction.

Key 21 symbolizes the new order of knowledge made possible by the perfected body of an adept. In this perfected organism, the new creature lives in a different world because he possesses a different inner mechanism for perceiving that world. Adepts understand the universe is continuous with and inseparable from their body. Identified with the Central Presence, they sense directly that the entire universe is their greater body. This is "cosmic consciousness."

We are keenly aware that no words of ours can convey the experience itself. Nevertheless, we want you to understand that this is a genuine experience. Testimony for this is abundant. It is what Buddha meant by Nirvana. Please note that one metaphor Buddha employed for Nirvana is the "Holy City."

The foundation of the city is the vital soul seated in Yesod. The One Ego is the "Lamb." The One Ego is the LIGHT. The One Ego manifests in the Administrative Intelligence, the greatest because it is the servant of all.

To know this is the goal of occult practice. The knowledge is incommunicable, but it is the quintessence of certitude. Every seer bears witness to this, and every seer knows himself to be a cosmic servant and knows himself to be a participant in the cosmic administration.

The new creatures are centered within the Cosmic Heart. Their perception of the universe includes knowledge of powers hidden from the gaze of ordinary humans. This perception enables them to use the powers of clear vision. Their life rests on no material basis. On the contrary, they are in union with the spiritual foundation of physical existence.

Yet they have gained no power not available to the unenlightened but know the meaning of the saying: "The Kingdom of Spirit is embodied in my flesh."

We purposely refrain from further vain attempts to describe this state of being. Nevertheless, to those who approach the Great

Work's completion, what we have written may carry a faint intimation of the glory of the actual realization.

That every reader of these words will someday know what we cannot tell is certain. This final realization is the ultimate destiny of every human personality. "We shall all be changed," wrote St. Paul. "If I am lifted up, I will draw all men unto me." There can be no exceptions. The creative process is successful. In it, there is no place for even a single failure. We shall be like him, for we shall all see him, the Divine Self, as he truly is.

APPENDIX 1 – 32 Paths in Hebrew

These translations are an expansion of the text given in the previous chapters.

1st Path

The 1st Path is the Marvelous Intelligence (Sekhel Mufla). It is the Light of the Primordial Mind. It is the 1st Glory. No creature can attain its essence.

הנתיב	הראשין	נקרא	שכל	מופלא
Path	The First	is	Consciousness	Marvelous
	1	called	Intelligence	פלא
	principal			wonderful
	supreme			Title of Kether

ו'ס'ע	והוא	אור	מישכל	קדמון
The highest	It is	light	Mind	ancient
crown			Intelligence	

והוא	כבוד	ראשון	אין	כל
It is	honor	First	not, no	all
	respect		nothing	
			without	

בריה	יכולה	ל-עמוד	על	מציאתו
Briah	can	stand	on	essence
Creation		platform	about	תמצית
נברא			to	summary
living creature(s)				essence, juice, lifeblood

קדמון - ancient, primitive, ancestor, eastern

מצת – igniter, spark, glow

The Second Path is that of the Illuminating Intelligence (Sekhel Maz'hir). It is the Crown of Creation. It is the Splendor of the Unity(s) and exalted above every head. The Masters of Reception call it the Second Glory.

הנתיב	ה-ב	הוא׳	נקרא
The Path	The "2" second	It	is called

שכל	מזהיר	ו-הוא	כתר
Consciousness Intelligence	Shining Radiant Illumination	& It is	*Kether* Crown

ה-בריאה	ו-זהר	ה-אחדות	השוה
Briah Creation	*Zohar* & Splendor	*ha-Achadot* The Unity(s)	It is

ה-מתנשא	ל-כל	ל-ראש	ו-הוא
exalted towering	every to all	head top, chief	& It

נקרא	כפי	בעלי	ה-קבלה
is called	by	Masters Kabbalists Masters of Reception	קבל receive

כבוד	שני		
glory	second		

284

The 3rd Path is Sanctifying Intelligence (Sekhel HaKudash). It is the foundation of Primordial Wisdom. It is called the Faithful Faith. It is the basis of faith (Amen) and the Father of Faith. By its power, Faith emanates (*Atziluth*).

הנתיב	ה-שלישי	נקרא	שכל
Path	the 3, 3rd	is called	Intelligence
			Consciousness

ה-קודש	ו-הוא	יסוד	ה-חכמה
The Holy	& it is	*Yesod*	*Chokmah*
Sanctity		Foundation	Wisdom

ה-קדומה	הנקרא	אמונה	אומן
The Ancient	is called	faith	Artisan
Primordial		confidence	craftsman
Original		honesty	educator

ו-שרשיה	אמן	ו-הוא	אב
& its roots	*Amen*	& It is	father
שירש	Faithfulness		
basis	Firm		
origin	found true		

ה-אמונה	שמכחו	ה-אמונה	נאצלת
The Faith	מכח	The Faith	Noble
trust	by its power		אצילות
	By virtue of		*Atziluth*
Atziluth – World of Fire.			Emanation

The Fourth Path is the Fixed or Immutable Intelligence (Sekhel Kavua). From it, all spiritual powers emanate as the most subtle emanations. Their powers are from the Original Emanation.

ה-נתיב	ה-רביעי	נקרא	שכל
the path	the 4, 4th	is called	Intelligence

קבוע	ונקרא	כן	שממנו
Fixed, constant	& called	yes	from which
Permanent		so	
immutable			
regular, steady			

מת-אצלים	כל	חכתות	ה-רחניות
Emanation	all	powers	רחן
		forces	spiritualization

ב-דקות	ה-אצילות	שמת-אצילות	אלו
subtlety	*Atziluth* - Emanation		These
fineness			They

מאלה	ב-כח	ה-מאציל	ה-קדמון
From these	force	אציל	Ancient
those	power	Emanation	Primordial
	strength		Original

דק – thin, lean, fine, delicate, sensitive, minute (time), dust, fine cloth, heaven (poetical).

The 5th Path is called Root Intelligence (Sekhel Nishrash). It is the essence of unity(s). Its essence of Binah (Intelligence, Understanding) emanates from the Original Wisdom's refuge (Chokmah).

ה-נתיב	ה-חמישי	נקרא	שכל
The Path	the 5, 5th	is called	Intelligence
			Consciousness

נשרש	ו-נקרא	כן	מפני
root, basis	& called	so	because
foundation			

שהוא	עצם	ה-אחדות	השוה
It is	essence	unity(s)	That

ו-הוא	המיוהד	ב-עצם	ה-בינה
& it is	not a word	essence	*Binah*
	מיועד		Understanding
	intended		
	designated		

ה-נאצלת	מגדר	החכמה	ה-קדומה
Atziluth	enclosure	Chokmah	Ancient
Emanation	גדר	Wisdom	Primordial
	to fence,		Original
	enclose		
	refuge		

The 6th Path is the Differentiating Influx Intelligence (Sekhel Shefa Nivdal). It emanates its blessing in abundance, uniting everything in its essence.

שכל	נקרא	ה-ששי	ה-נתיב
Intelligence	is called	sixth	The Path

ו-הוא	ה-אצילות	נבדל	שפע
& It is	Atziluth	to separate	influx
	Emanation	discern,	
	World of	divide	
	Fire	distinguish	
		distinct	
	בדל - to differentiate		
להבדיל - to separate day from night. Genesis 1:4.			

כל	על	ה-שפע	משפיע
all	on	influx	influencing
everything			giving in abundance

ב-עצמו	ה-מתאחדות	ה-בריכות	
in its essence	unite, uniting	Blessings	
	אחד	ברך	
	One (1)	To bless	

7th Path

The 7th Path is the Hidden Intelligence (Sekhel Nistar). It is the splendor that illuminates all intellectual powers visible to the mind's eye and contemplation of faith.

ה-נתיב	ה-שביעי	נקרא	שכל
The Path	7th	is called	Intelligence

נסתר	ו-נקרא	כן	מפני
hidden	& called	so	because
latent			
occult			

שהוא	זוהר	מזהיר	ל-כל
that is	*Zohar*	bright	to all
	radiant	shining	For all
	Splendor		
	זהר		
	to shine		

ה-כחות	ה-שכליים	ה-נראים	ב-עין
the Power(s)	Intellectual	the visible	eye
Force(s)	Rational	apparent, seen	

ה-שכל	ו-ב-רעיון	ה-אמונה	
The mind	and-of-thought	the Faith	
Intelligence	imagination		
	contemplation		
	idea, concept		
	desire		

The 8th Path is called the Whole or Perfect Intelligence (Sekhel Shalom). It is the Original Plan. There is no root where it can dwell except in the chamber of Gedulah (Greatness) from which its essence emanates.

שכל	נקרא	השמיני	ה-נתיב
Intelligence	is called	8	The Path

מפני	כן	ונקרא	שלם
because	so	& called	whole
			see below

ה-קדמות	תכונת	שהוא
Antiquity, Days of Old	attribute	It is
original	plan	that is
Primordial	trait	

שורש	לו	אין	אשר
root	to it	no	There
origin	if	not	that
basis	Oh that!		which

אם	כי	בו	ל-ה-תיישב
except	because	to it	ישב
	see below		to sit, dwell

מעצם	ה-נאצלים	ה-גדולה	ב-חדרי
essence	Atzileem	Gedulah	room
	Emanation	greatness	chamber
		Magnificence	bridal chamber

שלם – whole, entire, intact, complete, integral, unhewn, full, perfect, total, safe, unharmed, healthy true, faithful, peaceful.

כי – for, because, yet, but, as, if, in case, while, when, through, although, since, only.

9th Path

The 9th Path is the Pure Intelligence (Sekhel Tahor). It purifies the Sephiroth (numbers). It tests the law and repairs the pattern. They act in unison without the loss of their separate (unique) glow.

שכל	נקרא	ה-תשיעי	ה-נתיב
Intelligence	is called	ninth	The Path

לפי	כן	ו-נקרא	טהור
because	so	& called	pure
	yes		clean

ו-מבחין	את ה-ספירות	מטהר	שהוא
מבחן	Sephiroth	purifier	It is
test	numbering	purifies	
	counting	to be cleansed	

ו-תוכן	תבניתם	גזירת	ו-מבהיק
תכן	תבנית	גזרה	glowing?
& design	pattern, image	law	מבנה
	בנה	decree	structure
	establish, repair		building

מבלי	מיוחדות	שהן	אחדותם
without	אחדות	to be hot	their unity
	unity	to glow	oneness
		שהן	
		grace, favor	

את – This word indicates that	ו-פירוד	קצוץ
the next word in the sentence is	נפרד	chopped
a direct object.	separate	curtailment

10th Path

The 10th Path is Scintillating Intelligence (Sekhel Mit.notz.etz). It is exalted and sits on the throne of Binah (Understanding). It illuminates the splendor of all the lights and causes an influx of increase from the Prince of Face (Tiphareth).

ה-נתיב	ה-עשירי	נקרא	שכל
The Path	tenth	is called	Consciousness
מתנוצץ	ו-נקרא	כן	שהוא
Shining	& called	so	that is
מתצנץ		yes	
Scintillating			
מפני	מתעלה	ו-יושב	על
because	exalted - העלה	& sits	on
כסא	ה-בינה	ו-מאיר	ב-זוהר
seat	*Binah*	illuminate	*Zohar*
throne - כס	Understanding	shine	splendor,
	Intelligence	brightness	radiant
ה-מאורות	כולם	ו-משפיע	שפע
אור	everyone	influx	influx
fire		influence	abundance
illumination		motivate	wealth
ריבוי	ל-שר	ה-פונים	
רוה	Prince	פנים	
increase	captain	face	
multiply	ruler, noble	appearance	

293

The 11th Path is the Shining Consciousness (Shekel M'tzuk.tzach). It is truly the essence of the veil which arranges the sequence of the stars. It assigns the Paths their relationships. And (it) stands before the Cause of Causes (A title of Kether, the Crown – the 1st Path).

ה-נתיב	אחד	עשר	שכל
The Path	1	10	Intelligence

מצוחצח	ו-נקרא	כן	מפני
shining	& called	rightly	because
scintillating		true	

שהיא	עצם	ה-פרגוד	ה-מסודר
that is	essence	the veil	the arrangement
	bone	curtain	the ordered
	substance	screen	

פרגוד is related to פרכת, *parocheth* (curtain of the Ark of the Law).

ב-סדר	ה-מערכה	ו-הוא	יחס
Seder	the array	and it (he)	assign
in succession	arrangement	*Hu* – Kether's	attribute
sequence	disposition of	divine name	pedigree
series	the stars		relationship

ה-נתנת	ל-עמוד	ב-פני	ה-עילות עילת
the paths	to stand	in front	Cause of causes
	a pole	before	
		to face	

The 12th Path is the Glowing [Transparent[1]] Consciousness (Sekhel Bahir). It is the essence of the Great Wheel (the zodiac). It is called the Visualizer (Chaz.chaz.it). It is the source of vision of the prophets and those who see apparitions.

ה-נתיב	שנים	עשר	נקרא
The Path	2	10	is called

שכל	בוער	מפני	שהוא
Consciousness	glowing	because	that is
Intelligence	burning		
באיר – No such word. Rabbi Kaplan translates, "Glowing."			

עצם	ה-אופן	ה-גדלה	ו-נקרא
essence	*Ophan*	the great	& called
bone	The wheel	magnificence	
substance		increase	

חזחזית	פי	מקים	מוצא
Chaz.chaz.it	Transitive	place, spot	Source, Origin
Visualizer	verb[2]	dwelling-place	Fountain
חזית		seat	way out
Seeing, prophecy, revelation		location	utterance, edict

חזיון	ה-חוזים	ב-מראה	
vision	Prophets[3]	appearance, vision	
	חוזה	sight, view, seeing	
	prophet	mirror	
		shown, displayed	

[1] Some writers translate this word as Transparent. Transparent is
ברור. In Alcalay's *English to Hebrew*, p. 1582, glowing is בוער.
Either could be correct.

[2] A **transitive verb** has two characteristics. First, it is an action
verb expressing a doable activity like kick, want, paint, write, eat,
clean, etc. Second, it must have a direct object, something or
someone who receives the verb's action.

[3] Prophets are spelled with two Cheth (ח) in the original text.
Therefore, I changed the first Cheth to Heh (ה).

The 13th *Path* is the Unity Directing Consciousness (*Sekhel Man.hig Ha.Achdut*). It (*Hu*) is the essence of Glory and the reward of the spiritual ones.

ה-נתיב	שלשה	עשר	נקרא
The Path	3	10	is called
שכל	מנהיג	ה-אחדות	מפני
Intelligence	leader	the unity(s)	because
Consciousness	director	uniting	
	directing	harmony	
שהוא	עצם	ה-כבוד	ו-הוא
It is	essence	the glory	and it (he)
that is	substance	respect	*Hu* –
	bone	majesty	divine
		honor	name of
		importance	Kether
תשלום	אמתת	ה-רוחניים	ה-אחדים
reward	truth	Spiritual(s)	"the ones"
completion	verify		the others
payment	confirm		beings
consummation	authenticate		things
	prove right		unity (s)

The 14th Path is Illuminating Intelligence (Sekhel Meir). It is the essence of electricity (Chashmal). It teaches the fundamentals of the secret mysteries of the Holy Sanctuary and its plan.

נקרא	עשר	ארבעה	ה-נתיב
is called	10	4	The Path

שהיא	מפני	מאיר	שכל
It is	because	luminous	Intelligence
that is		Illuminating	Consciousness
		light	
		brightness	

על	ו-ה-מורה	ה-חשמל	עצם
of [2]	& the teacher	Chashmal [1]	essence
	instruction	shining, amber	substance
		electricity	bone
		substance	

ו-תכונתם	ה-קדש	יסודות	רזי
& its plan	the sanctuary	basics	mysteries
תכונה [3]	holy	foundations	secret(s)
	to be consecrated	fundamental	רז
	Holy Temple		secret

[1] "speaking silence" – Kaplan

[2] על – on, upon, over, near, to, unto, towards, against; with, together, because; yoke, burden, servitude.

[3] quality, character, trait, plan, astronomy, treasures (biblical).

The 15th Path is Stable Intelligence (Sekhel Ma'amid). From the pure darkness, it stabilizes the essence of Creation (Briah). The Masters say, "wrapped it in thick darkness." – Job 38:9.

ה-נתיב	החמשה	עשר	נקרא
The Path	5	10	is called
שכל	מעמיד	ו-נקרא	כן
Intelligence	stable	is called	Yes, truly
מפני	שהוא	מעמיד	עצם
because	It is	stability	essence
		base	substance
ה-בריאה	כ-ערפלי	טהור	ו-בעלי
Briah, creation	darkness	pure	masters
2nd World of	foggy		
Creation	gloom		
העיון	אמרו	כי	הוא
Theory	they said	because	Hu
עיוני			It, he
Theoretical			
ה-ערפל	ו-זהו	ו-ערפל	ה-תולתו
darkness	and - that is	fog	curly
gloom	this is		band
wrapped it in thick darkness			

ערפלי – According to Alcalay, Lower Sky in the Kabbalah

The 16th Path is Eternal Intelligence (Sekhel Nitz.chi). It is the pleasure (Eden) of the Glory. There is no Glory like it (beneath it). It is called the Garden of Eden, prepared for the Merciful Ones (Saints).

ה-נתיב	ששה	עשר	נקרא
The Path	6	10	is called

שכל	נצחי	ו-נקרא	כן
Intelligence	eternal	is called	truly
Consciousness	infinite		

מפני	שהוא	עדון	ה-כבוד
because	It is	*Eden*, garden	The glory
	as it is	pleasure, delight	honor
		time period, era	

שאין	כבוד	ל-מטה	
There is no	glory	like it	
		beneath	

הימנה	כמו	שהוא	שם
There	same as, like	It is	*Shem* – name

והוא	הנקרא	גן	עדן
Hu, and it	called	garden	Eden

חמוכן	ל-**חסדים**	חסד	
prepared	reward of the	*Chesed*- Mercy, grace, love	
ready		חסד	
		4th Sephiroth	

The 17th Path is Perceptive Intelligence (Sekhel Ha.Her.gesh). It is prepared for the Faithful Ones (Saints) so they are clothed with the Holy Spirit. It is called the Foundation (Yesod) of Beauty (Tiphareth) and is placed among the Supernals (upper realms).

ה-נתיב	שבעה	עשר	נקרא
The Path	7	10	is called
שכל	ה-הרגש	ו-הוא	מוכן
Intelligence	the senses	and it/he	prepared
Consciousness	excite	Hu	ready
	perceptive		
	feeling		
ל-חסידי	ה-אמונה	ל-ה-תלבשא	בו
Merciful Ones	faith, belief	to dress	with
Saints	Confidence	clothed	
ב-רוה	קדושה	ו-חוא	נקרא
Rauch	holy, blessing	and it/he	is called
soul, spirit	purification	Hu	
Wind, breath	sanctification		
יסוד	ה-תפארת	ב-מעמד	ה-עליונים
Yesod	Tiphareth	at the place	The upper(s)
foundation	the beauty	standing, erected	Height
Bbasis, source	glory, honor	candidate	Supernal
element	magnificence	nominee	supremacy

301

The 18th Path is called the Intelligence of the House of Influx (Shekel bet ha-shefa). From investigations [walls], a secret is transmitted/attracted to all who dwell/cleave to its shadow. Those who walk the 18th Path bind themselves to investigating the substance (reality) transmitted (emanating) from Cause of Causes.

ה-נתיב	שמונה	נקרא	שכל
The Path	8	is called	Intelligence
בית	ה-שפע	ו-מתוך	חקירותו ¹
house	influx	from, of	probe
dwell	Influence	out of	investigate
	abundance	since, as	חקר
			search, inquiry
מושכים	רז	והירה	המתלוננים
attracting	secret	?	?
משך	mystery	העבר	יתלוננים
attract		transmit	he-will-rest
			Ps. 90:1
ב-עלו	ו-הדבקים	ב-חקירות	ממשותו
in its	& cleave	probe	reality
(shadow)	bind, join	investigate	effect
	cling, glue		Substance
מעילת	העילות		
cause	of causes		

¹ הקירותו – It's walls. Notice the meaning of the word is changed by using Heh (ה) instead of Cheth (ח).

The 19th Path is the Intelligence of the Secret of All Spiritual Activities (Sekhel Sod HaPaulot Haruchniot Kulam). It is the influx that permeates from the Supreme Blessing and the Glory of the Most High.

ה-נתיב	תשעה	נקרא	שכל
The Path	9	is called	Intelligence

סוד	ה-פעולות	ה-רוחניות	כולם
secret	the actions	Spiritual(s)	all
	activities	רוח	everyone
	accomplish	*Rauch*	
		spirit, breath	

מפני	שהוא	ה-שפע	ה-מתפשט
because	It is	influx	pervasive
		abundance	permeates
		18th Path	פשט
			stretch, extend

בו	מהברכה	ה-עליונה	ו-ה-כבוד
from	blessing	the height	& the glory
with	ברך	top	respect
	to bless, thank	supreme	glory

ה-מעולה	מעלה - rise, elevated
the excellent	
מעלה	עול - height

303

The 20th Path is the Intelligence of Will (Sekhel HaRatzon). It is the trait from which everything is formed. Through this consciousness, everyone can know the essence of the Original Wisdom.

שכל	נקרא	העשרים	ה-נתיב
Intelligence	is called	20	The Path

תכונת	שהוא	מפני	ה-רצון
attribute, trait	It is	because	the will
characteristic			goodwill
plan, astronomy			desire

ו-ב-זה	כולם	ה-יצורים	כל
&-in-this	all	fabrication,	all
Through this	everyone	form(s)	everyone
This is		formed	

יצירה — *Yetzirah* – The World of Formation

מציאות	יודע	כל	ה-שכל
existence	know	all	consciousness
essence	knowing		Intelligence

ה-קדומה		ה-חכמה
the ancient		*Chokmah*
original, primordial		2nd Sephiroth
קדם - Ancient Days		wisdom
קדמון - ancient, primitive, ancestor;		intelligence
eastern		science
		insight

The 21st Path is Seeking and Delightful Intelligence (Sekhel HaChafutz HaMevukash). It receives the divine influx to bless all, everyone.

ה-נתיב	אחד	ו-עשרים	נקרא
The Path	1	and 20	is called

שכל	ה-חפץ	ה-מבוקש	מפני
Intelligence	wish, desire	בקש	because
Consciousness	delight	to ask, desire	
	have affection for	seek, to search	
	find pleasure in		

שהוא	מקבל	שפע	ה-אלהות
It is	receives	influx	divinity
	accepted	18th Path	divine

כדי	ל-חשפיע	מברכת	ל-כל
in order to	to influence	bless	to all
so that	to bestow	ברק	
to the extent	שפע - 18th Path	to bless	

הנמצאים	כולם		
found	all		
available	everyone		
discovered			

מצא – to find, find out, guess, catch, reach, overtake, discover, come upon, reveal, meet, encounter, happen, occur, and be sufficient.

The 22nd Path is Faithful Intelligence (Sekhel Ne'eman). It causes spiritual powers to multiply. The Spiritual Ones are drawn close through it, and all find shelter in its shadow.

ה-נתיב	שנים	ו-עשרים	נקרא
The Path	2	20	is called

שכל	נאמן	מפני	שבו
Intelligence	Faithful, sure	because	It is
Consciousness	Loyal, firm		
	trustworthy		

מתרבים	כחות	ה-רוחניות	כדי
multiply	power, force	spiritual(s)	through it
רבה	strength	רוח	
to increase	כח	*Rauch*	
enlarge	Resource	spirit	
cultivate	ability, riches	wind, breath	

להיותם	קרובים	ל-כל	ה-יתלוננים
to be	close, relation	to all	dwell?
היה	near, at hand		יתלוננים
exist, become	about		he-will-rest
come to pass	approximately		Ps. 90:1

ב-צילו	צל - shadow, shade, shelter, protection.
in his shadow	
shelter	

The 23rd Path is Sustaining Intelligence (Sekhel Kayam). It is the power sustaining all the Sephiroth.

ה-נתיב	שלשה	ו-עשרים	נקרא
The Path	3	20	is called

שכל	קיום	מפני	שהוא
Intelligence	sustaining	because	It is
Consciousness	subsistence		
	existence		
	observance		

כח	קיום	ל-כל	ה-ספירות
power	sustaining	to all	Sephiroth
strength, force	subsistence	for all	numbers
wealth, riches	existence		numerations
Resource	observance		counting
ability			

The 24th Path is Imaginative Intelligence (Sekhel Dimyoni). It gives a form to the imaginations of all Living Creatures.

ה-נתיב	ארבעה	ו-עשרים	נקרא
The Path	4	& 20	is called

שכל	דמיוני	מפני	שהוא
Intelligence	imaginative	because	It is
Consciousness	resemblance		It
	likeness		
	fantasy		

נותן	דמות	ל-כל	ה-דמיונים
נתן	likeness	to all	imaginations
gives	image	of all	
provides	figure		
dispense	character		

נבראים			
Living Creatures			

308

The 25th Path is Experimental Intelligence (Sekhel Nisyoni). It is the primary test through which all the Merciful Ones become skilled.

הנתיב	חמשה	ו-עשרים	נקרא
Path	5	20	is called

שכל	נסיוני	מפני	שהוא
Intelligence	Experimental	because	It is
Consciousness	trial, test		
	נסיון		
	trial, test		
	probation		

ה-נסיון	ה-קדמון	שבו	מנסה
the test	primary	through	experience
	primitive	which	skilled, tested
	ancient		tried out
	original		

ל-כל	ה-חסידים
to all	Merciful Ones
	Saints

The 26th Path is Regenerating Intelligence (Sekhel MeChudash). By it, the Blessed Holy One regenerates the World of Creation.

ה-נתיב	ששה	ו-עשרים	נקרא	שכל
The Path	6	20	is called	Intelligence

מחודש	מפני	קב "ה	ש"' ה	מחדש
renewed	because	Blessed Holy One		Innovator
regenerate		שם המפרש - ש"ה -		inventor
		The Ineffable Name		rejuvenation
		(God)		Title of God

בו	כל	ה-חדשים	ב-בריאת
By it	all	renew, revive, invent	in creation
		establish a new	making
		interpretation	world
			cosmos

ה-עולם	קב "ה		
the world	קודשא	בריך	הוא
universe	The Holy	Blessed be	He (*Hu*)
humanity	One		
space			
existence			
eternity, ages			
distant future			

The 27th Path is the Perceptible or Felt Intelligence (Sekhel Murgash). Through it, the senses of all living beings under the zodiac are excited.

ה-נתיב	שבעה	ו-עשרים	נקרא
The Path	7	20	is called
שכל	מורגש	ו-הוא	חומר
Intelligence	מרגש	& it	חמר
Consciousness	felt, perceived		material
	perceptible		element
			matter
מפני	שממנו	נבראו	ה-נבראים
because	from which	were created	נברא
	through	his creatures	living
		humanity	creature(s)
כל	מתחת	גלגל	ה-עליון
all	below, under	revolve	high, exalted
	beneath	zodiac	The Most High
		to cause	Title of God
		bring about	
ו-ה-רגשותם		רגש	
and the feelings		To be excited, to rage	
		Emotion, sense	

The 28th Path is called Natural Intelligence (Sekhel Mutba). It completes and perfects the nature of all that exists under the revolution of the Sun.

ה-נתיב	שמנה	ו-עשרים	נקרא
The Path	8	& 20	is called

שכל	מוטבע	מפני	שבו
Intelligence	מטבע	Because	It is
Consciousness	Innate, Inborn		
	natural		

נשלם	טבע	כל	ה-נמצים
completed	nature	all	נמצא
	character		existing
	element		available

מתחת	גלגל	ה-חמה	ב-שלימות
under	to cause	warmth	perfected
below		heat	In perfection
			שלום
	revolve	The Sun	complete
	circuit of the Sun		peace

312

29th Path of Qoph - ק

The 29th Path is Physical Intelligence (Sekhel Mugsham). It depicts and establishes the growth of all physical bodies incorporated under the Zodiac.

The Zodiac is an allusion to the Celestial Spheres of the ancients, the seven planets, plus the 8th sphere of the fixed stars.

הנתיב	תשעה	ו-עשרים	נקרא
Path	9	& 20	is called

שכל	מוגשם	מפני	שהוא
Intelligence	physical	because	It is
Consciousness	corporal		

מתאר	כל	גשם	שית-גשם [1]
Described	All	physical	incorporated
Depicted	every	body	
Portrayed			

תחת	תכונת	ה-גלגלים	ב-גידולים
Under	כון [2]	the revolutions	In growth
below	established	the zodiac	development
Instead		cycles, spheres	raising

[1] שית – to place, put, set, lay, fix, appoint, foundation, bottom, pit.

[2] כון – to be correct, proper, firm, established, clear, determined, ready, and prepared.

The 30th Path is called Collective or Inclusive Intelligence (Sekhel Kelali). Through it, astrologers study the laws governing the stars and the zodiac and perfect their knowledge. [Stars include the seven planets known to the ancients.]

נתיב	שלשים	נקרא	שכל
Path	30	is called	Intelligence

כללי	מפני	כוללים	הוברי
Collective	because of	comprehensive	Astrologers
Universal		inclusive	
General		including	
common		embracing	

שמים	ב-משפטיהם	ה-ככבים	וה-מזלות
Heavens	Justice	to shine	*Mazloth*
starry sky	Laws	ככב	Zodiac
	statutes	Star(s)	Fortunate
		Mercury	Lucky

עיונם	תשלומי	ידיעתם	ב- אופן
theoretical	completion	דעת	אופנים
speculative	payment	*Da'ath*	*Ophanim*
deep study		knowledge	wheels
reward		wisdom	Ezekiel 10:20

גלגלים
wheels, sphere
to revolve, to cause

The 31st Path is Perpetual Intelligence (Sekhel Tamidi). It regulates all the cyclic forces that form the revolutions of the stars and planets (Mazloth).

ה-נתיב	אחד	ו-שלשים	נקרא
The Path	1	and 30	is called
שכל	תמידי	מפני	שהוא
Intelligence	continuous	Because of	It is
Consciousness	consistent		
	perpetual		
כלל	כחות	כל	ה-גלגלים
rule	Power(s)	all	to cause
regulates	Forces		to revolve
principle			wheels
whole			sphere
ו-מזלות	ו-ה-צורות	ו-**משפטי**הם	
Mazloth	& the form(s)	משפט	
zodiac	צור	(and their) Law	
	shapes	theorem	
	to mold, form	their judgments, Justice	
	to bind, wrap	rock, fortress, refuge	

The 32nd Path is Serving Intelligence (Sekhel Ne'evad). It repairs (Tikun) all the seven planets' operations and keeps them in their orbits.

נתיב	שנים	ו-שלשים	נקרא
Path	2	& 30	is called

שכל	נעבד	מפני	שהוא
Intelligence	serving	because	It
Consciousness	work		It is
	slave		
	worship		

מתוקן	לכל	חמשתמשים	ב-עבודת
repairs	To all	?	work(s)
תוקן		תמשים	Operations
Tikun		realize	
fixed			
repair			

שבעה	ככבי	לכת	ל-חבלם [1]
7	planets	to go	to orbit, orbiting
	stars		חבלים
			ropes, rigging

[1] חבלם - The ideas of ropes and rigging imply gravity in the context of this text. Therefore I translated the word as "orbit."

APPENDIX 2

Oedipus Aegyptiacus T.2, Volume 1 – pp. 312 – 316

By Athanasius Kircher

And these are the 32 paths, which Rasbi and R. Ioseph Haaruch [רבי שמעון בן ירחאי] learn from the first chapter of Genesis, and the Hageonim confer each one of them their names, derived from their effects. Thus, let us add the name of each path taken from Pardes.[1]

1st Path

The 1st Path is called Admirable Intelligence, the Supreme Crown. As a matter of fact, it is the light that allows us to understand the beginning without beginning, and it is the first glory. No creature can obtain its essence; namely, it is a hidden Intelligence, unclear to anything which is outside it.

Aleph (א) is the beginning and the origin of everything, and that is so because Aleph (א) is the model of all letters, and all the paths are contained in it, but universally; from such thing, through metathesis, it is said *pehleh* (פלא), namely, "admirable," which, due to the retrograde meaning, it is the same as (אלף) Aleph, according to that verse: "and His name will be Wonderful, Mighty God, etc."

For us, a child is born. To us, a son is given, and the government will be on his shoulders. And he will be called Wonderful Counselor, Mighty God, Everlasting Father, Prince of Peace. – Isaiah 9:6.

2nd Path

The 2nd Path is Shining Intelligence. It is the crown of creation and the splendor of the most Universal Unity, which has been raised above any individual, and it is called the "second glory" by Cabalists. So, it is called the "second glory" because, being the origin of the entire creation, it is more known than the immediately previous one, that is [אין סוף] Ain Soph, the hidden Intelligence. So this path is also called "the way of adjustment," Radak[2] [David Kimhi] so, in this passage of Yetzirah.

3rd Path

The 3rd Path is called Glorifying Intelligence, and it is the fundament of primary knowledge, which is called the "creator of faith" and its "roots"[אמן], and it is the "mother of faith" because faith stems from its power. It corresponds to the third Sephira or to the third measure, which is called Binah [בינה], or "Intelligence," because, through it, there is a fulfillment of knowledge for all measures. However, see the book "Baresitich Rabba," which discourses profusely about such matters.

4th Path

The 4th Path is called Intelligence of "Destination" or of "Guidance" because all the spiritual virtues, by their subtility, stem from it, as they are brought towards it, as being a goal, by the higher Intelligences; from it, one thing comes out from the other, by virtue of the Supreme Crown, and it is called "ideal flux."

5th Path

The 5th Path is called Radical Intelligence because it is the very Universal Unity, which aggregates itself with that Binah [בינה] Intelligence, which stems from the most internal parts of the primary knowledge. The virtues, taken from the higher paths to this fifth path, and herein clinging, have become equal when they are carried from this path to the inferior ones, they pass, and they are transformed, according to the different behavior of men, into clemency or into a severe judgment; see Pardes, about such matter.

6th Path

The 6th Path is called Intelligence of the Mediating Influence because the emanations' flux is multiplied in it. It makes it so that this inflow shall flow in all containers of blessings united in it. This one is called the "path of water."

7th Path

The 7th Path is called Hidden Intelligence because it is the splendor shining on all intellectual virtues, which are perceived by the eyes of our reason and by the contemplation of our faith. It is called "hidden" because it is not understood but through the Intelligences of the Measures. It is distinguished from the first path because it is incomprehensible, while this one is comprehensible. It is called the "path of intellectual entities."

8th Path

The 8th Path is called Absolute and Perfect Intelligence because it is the primary organization; it does not have roots adhering unless in the most internal parts of the Sephira, called "Magnificence," and stems from its very essence. It is said the "Path of things living in water."

9th Path

The 9th Path is called Pure Intelligence because it purifies measures, approves and corrects the destruction of their appearance. It establishes the Unity of the things that are united to it with no amputation or division. It is said the "path of purification of things."

10th Path

The 10th Path is called Sparkling Intelligence because it has been exalted above every individual and is located on the throne of Binah. It emits the flare of all lights and acts so that it gives license to the "head of images." It is said the "Path of the variety of things."

11th Path

The 11th Path is called Luminous Intelligence because it is the curtain placed by the disposition and order of the higher and lower paths, and it is a sort of dignity granted to it to stay in front of the Cause of Causes.

12th Path

The 12th Path is called "Intelligence of Limpidity" because it is the very appearance of magnificence, and it is said to be the place from which the vision stems for those who see with apparitions. So, through it, a prophecy is obtained, and we reach the Supreme Chariot.

13th Path

The 13th Path is called Inductive Intelligence of Unity because it is the essence of glory and perfects the truth of each spiritual thing. All the paths that unite to the Supreme Unity join themselves through this 13th path. In fact, *achad* [אחד], interpreted as a number, gives 13.

14th Path

The 14th Path is called Illuminating Intelligence because it is "Chasmal," the founder of mysteries and fundament of sanctity and the organization of such matter. It is said to be the path of secrets existing in created beings.

15th Path

The 15th Path is called Constituting Intelligence because it constitutes the creation "in the darkness of the world," The philosophers said that it is the very darkness about which Job talks in the Scripture: "and the dark cloud its wrapping." It is also said the path of the aperture of light.

16th Path

The 16th Path is called Triumphing and Eternal Intelligence since it is the very joy of glory, which is similar to it, and it is called the Paradise of delight, which has been prepared for honest people. It is also said the path of victory against evil geniuses.

17th Path

The 17th Path is called Disposing Intelligence, which prepares the Christian faith for the devout so that, through it, they shall be covered by the Holy Spirit, and it is said to be the fundament of beauty by the condition of Supreme entities. Moreover, it supervises all superior and inferior forms.

18th Path

The 18th Path is called the Intelligence or the House of Influence because by the middle of its meticulous research mysteries are drawn, as long as the obscure meanings which are hidden in its shadows, and the things, which are interlinked to its ipseity, are drawn from the Cause of the Causes.

19th Path

The 19th Path is called the Intelligence of the Secret, or of all Spiritual Activities, because an influx is spread for it from the highest benediction [or recipient] and by the noblest or supreme glory. It is the path of influx towards all Measures [Sephiroth].

20th Path

The 20th Path is called the Intelligence of Will because it is the organization of every created being, and through it, the existence of primordial knowledge becomes very known. It is the path of the mysteries of knowledge.

21st Path

The 21st Path is called Intelligence of Delight of the Desired Matter because It receives the divine influence so that it shall penetrate, by its blessing, every existing thing.

22nd Path

The 22nd Path is called Faithful Intelligence because spiritual virtues have been deposited into its hands and nurtured through it so that they shall be close to those who live under its shadow.

23rd Path

The 23rd Path is called Established Intelligence because it is the virtue of consistency for all numerations [Sephiroth].

24th Path

The 24th Path is called Imaginative Intelligence because it grants similarity to each affinity among the created things.

25th Path

The 25th Path is called Tempting Intelligence because it is the primary temptation by which God tests pious people.

26th Path

The 26th Path is called Renewing Intelligence because, through it, all the things, which have been renewed during the creation of the world, are renewed

27th Path

The 27th Path is called Provocative Intelligence, and it is the matter from which all the things produced under the Supreme Sphere have been created and their movements.

28th Path

The 28th Path is called Natural Intelligence because, through it, the nature of every existing thing under the Sun's orbit has been perfected.

29th Path

The 29th Path is called Corporal Intelligence because it molds each body, which is materialized under the organization of all the Spheres and their increments.

30th Path

The 30th Path is called Deductive Intelligence because Astrologers deduct their speculations by evaluating the stars and celestial signs. They derive their knowledge's perfection from observing their revolving motions.

31st Path

The 31st Path is called Deductive Intelligence because it also comprehends all the effects of the Spheres, the celestial signs, their forms (or images), and their configuration and evaluation.

32nd Path

The 32nd Path is called Aiding Intelligence because it quickly points toward all seven planets' operations and their parts.

And these are the 32 paths of knowledge, which proceed from the Supreme Knowledge, and Binah, namely the Intelligence, actualizes them. These things are called "Intelligences" because they direct, illuminate, stimulate and prepare the scholar of Mosaic law to search and love God, hidden in all things, as well as for obtaining, tidily, the union with God and the adherence to this dear entity, on which the entire human happiness is based. This is the operative usage of these paths. Therefore, when Cabalists want to examine God through some certain path of natural things, firstly, having predisposed great zeal and preparation, they consult the 32 verses of the first chapter of Genesis, namely the created beings' paths. Then, having made certain prayers, they ask God, through the name Elohim (אלהים), so that He shall grant the appropriate light for the investigation of the decided path; moreover, having made several rites, they eventually persuade themselves of having obtained the light of knowledge, as long as they have dedicated themselves to the investigation, through a pure heart, indestructible faith, and zealous affection. And so that the present speech shall have a greater effect, they use, at most, the name of 42 letters, not happening without awe, which never lacks; because it has been taken from the first and the last verse of the Mosaic law, they think that they have, in this way, the highest and mysterious ability to obtain the thing which desires through it. If the following matter seems good, shall the reader consult the third paragraph about God's name made of 42 letters to better understand this passage. First, however, the more detailed discussion below is about the way of pronouncing it.

[1] **"Pardes"** refers to (types of) approaches to biblical exegesis in rabbinic Judaism or interpretation of text in Torah study. The term, sometimes also spelled **PaRDeS**, is an acronym formed from the same initials of the following four approaches:

- <u>Peshat</u> (פְּשָׁט) – "surface" ("straight") or the literal (direct) meaning.[1]
- **R**emez (רֶמֶז) – "hints" or the deep (allegoric: hidden or symbolic) meaning beyond just the literal sense.
- **D**erash (דְּרַשׁ) – from Hebrew *darash*: "inquire" ("seek") – the comparative (<u>midrashic</u>) meaning, as given through similar occurrences.
- Sod (סוֹד) (pronounced with a long O as in 'lore') – "secret" ("mystery") or the esoteric/mystical meaning, as given through inspiration or revelation.

- Wikipedia

[2] **David Kimhi** (<u>Hebrew</u>: דוד קמחי, also Kimchi or Qimḥi) (1160–1235), also known by the Hebrew acronym as the **RaDaK** (רד"ק) (Rabbi David Kimhi), was a medieval rabbi, biblical commentator, philosopher, and grammarian.

- Wikipedia

APPENDIX 3

Divine Names of the Planetary Sephiroth

In Chapter 16, Case gives these instructions.

Besides the Tarot, colors and musical notes are related to chakras. The divine names corresponding to the Sephiroth from Binah to Yesod inclusive may be employed to rouse the planetary centers' activity. They should be intoned on a monotone or use the musical notes associated with the planetary force. For example, Elohim (pronounced ale-oh-heem, with the accent on the last syllable) is intoned to the note A for the center at the base of the spine.

I unpacked this paragraph into the tables below.

Sephiroth	Planet	Color	Note	Geometric Figure	Divine Name
Binah	Saturn	Blue-violet deep indigo	A	Triangle	IHVH Elohim יהוה אלהים
Chesed	Jupiter	Violet	A#	Square	El - אל
Geburah	Mars	Red	C	Pentagon Pentagram	Elohim Gibor אלהים גובר
Tiphareth	The Sun	Orange	D	Hexagram	IHVH[1] יהוה
Netzach	Venus	Green	F#	Septagon	IHVH Tzabaoth יהוה צבאות
Hod	Mercury	Yellow	E	Octagon	Elohim Tzabaoth אלהים טבאות
Yesod	The Moon	Blue	G#	Nonagon or Enneagon	Shaddai El Chai שדי אל חי

= sharp

[1] Western Schools use IHVH Eloah va-Daath as the divine name of Tiphareth. Qabalists use IHVH.

The divine names can also be sung, with the proper note for each letter.

Binah – Saturn								
I	H	V	H	A	L	H	I	M
י	ה	ו	ה	א	ל	ה	י	ם
F	C	C#	C	E	F#	C	F	G#
Yod	Heh	Wah	Heh	a	yl	he	ee-m	

Chesed Jupiter	
A	L
א	ל
E	F#
a	yl

Geburah – Mars								
A	L	H	I	M	G	B	V	R
א	ל	ה	י	ם	ג	ב	ו	ר
E	F#	C	F	G#	G#	E	C#	D
A	yl	hee		em	gee	boo		r

Tiphareth – The Sun											
I	H	V	H	A	L	V	H	V	D	O	Th
י	ה	ו	ה	א	ל	ו	ה	ו	ד	ע	ת
F	C	C#	C	E	F#	C#	C	C#	F#	A	A#
Yod	Heh	Wah	Heh	A	yl	v-ah		vah	D-aa-th		

Netzach – Venus								
I	H	V	H	Tz	B	A	V	Th
י	ה	ו	ה	צ	ב	א	ו	ת
F	C	C#	C	A#	E	E	C#	A#
Yod	Heh	Wah	Heh	Tza	bah		oo-th	

Hod - Mercury									
A	L	H	I	M	Tz	B	A	V	Th
א	ל	ה	י	ם	צ	ב	א	ו	ת
E	F#	C	F	G#	A#	E	E	C#	A#
A	yl	he		em	Tza	bah		oo-th	

Yesod – The Moon							
Sh	D	I	A	L	Ch	I	
ש	ד	י	א	ל	ח	י	
C	F#	F	E	F#	D#	F	
Shah	dah	ee	A	yl	ch	ee	

Sephiroth	Divine Name		Meaning
	English	Hebrew	
Kether	E.hey.yeh hey	אהיה	I will be what I will be
Chokmah	Yah	יה or יהוה	God, Strength, Vastness
Binah	IHVH Elohim	יהוה אלהים	Lord God
Chesed	El	אל	God, Power
Geburah	Elohim Gibor	אלהים גובר	God of Strength
Tiphareth	IHVH	יהוה	Jehovah, the Lord God
Tiphareth	IHVH Eloah va-Daath	יהוה אלוה ודעת	God Manifest
Netzach	IHVH Tzabaoth	יהוה צבאות	Lord of Hosts
Hod	Elohim Tzabaoth	אלהים צבאות	God of Hosts
Yesod	Shaddai El Chai	שדי אל חי	Almighty God of Life
Malkuth	Adonai Ha Aretz	אדני הארץ	Lord of Earth

[1] Western Schools use IHVH Eloah va-Daath as the divine name of Tiphareth. Qabalists use IHVH.

APPENDIX 4 – PERFECT NUMBERS

The study of perfect numbers is ancient. The first recorded instance of their study was by Pythagoras and his followers. Their interest was in their mystical properties.

A perfect number is a number that is the sum of its divisors. The ancients called a divisor an 'aliquot parts' of a number. For example, the aliquot parts of 10 are 1, 2, and 5. Note that $1 = {}^{10}/_{10}$; $2 = {}^{10}/_{5}$; and $5 = {}^{10}/_{2}$. 10 is not an aliquot part of 10 since it is not a proper quotient (The number obtained by dividing one quantity by another) and is different from the number itself.

The four perfect numbers 6, 28, 496, and 8128 were known from ancient times. There is no record of these discoveries. These are:

$6 = 1 + 2 + 3$
$1 + \mathbf{2} = \mathbf{3}$
$6 = 2 \times 3$

$28 = 1 + 2 + 4 + 7 + 14 = 28$
$1 + 2 + \mathbf{4} = \mathbf{7}$
$4 \times 7 = 28$

$496 = 1 + 2 + 4 + 8 + 16 + 31 + 62 + 124 + 248 = 496$
$1 + 2 + 4 + 8 + \mathbf{16} = \mathbf{31}$
$16 \times 31 = 496$

$8,128 = 1 + 2 + 4 + 8 + 16 + 32 + \mathbf{64} + \mathbf{127} + 254 + 508 + 1016 + 2032 + 4064$
$1 + 2 + 4 + 8 + 16 + 32 + \mathbf{64} = \mathbf{127}$
$64 \times 127 = 8,128$

The first recorded mathematical result concerning perfect numbers, which is known, occurs in Proposition 36 of Book IX of Euclid's *Elements,* written around 300 BC.

Stated if $1 + 2 + 4 = 7$, which is prime. Then (the sum) $\times$ (the last) $= 7 \times 4 = 28$, which is a perfect number. Also, $1 + 2 + 4 + 8 + 16 = 31$ which is prime. Then $31 \times 16 = 496$ is a perfect number.

If we restate Euclid's rigorous proof in modern form:

If $\qquad 1 + 2 + 4 + \ldots + 2^{n-1} = 2^n - 1.$

Then: If for some $n > 1$, $2^n - 1$ is prime, then $2^{n-1}(2^n - 1)$ is a perfect number.

However, this did not stand the test of time. It was discovered later that if a number was of this form, it might be a candidate to be a perfect number but not always.

Please note that prime numbers of form $2^n - 1$ are called Mersenne Primes after Marin Mersenne, a French priest.

Nicomachus made the next significant study of perfect numbers of Gerasa. Around 100 C.E., Nicomachus wrote *Introductio Arithmetica,* which gives a classification of numbers based on perfect numbers. Nicomachus divides numbers into three classes, superabundant numbers (the sum of the divisors [aliquot parts] is greater than the number, deficient numbers (the sum of the aliquot parts is less than the number), and perfect numbers (the sum of their aliquot parts is equal to the number). He states:

Among simple even numbers, some are superabundant. Others are deficient: these two classes are two extremes opposed to one another; those that occupy the middle position between the two are

334

said to be perfect. And those who are said to be opposite to each other, the superabundant and the deficient, are divided in their condition, inequality, into the too much and the too little.

Note the moral terms that Nicomachus uses to describe the three sets of numbers:

In the case of too much, excess, superfluity, exaggerations, and abuse, in too little, it is produced wanting, defaults, privations, and insufficiencies. And in the case of those found between the too much and the too little, that is in equality, is produced virtue, measure, propriety, beauty, and things of that sort – of which the most exemplary form is that type of number which is called perfect.

Perfect numbers had a religious significance, namely that 6 is the days God took to create the world. It is said that God chose this number because it was perfect, and the next perfect number is 28, the number of days it takes the Moon to travel around the Earth. Saint Augustine (354-430) writes in *The City of God*:-

Six is a number perfect in itself, not because God created all things in six days; rather, the converse is true. God created all things in six days because the number is perfect...

Nicomachus goes on to describe certain results concerning perfect numbers. Those that stood the test of time are:

1.   All perfect numbers are even.
2.   All perfect numbers end in 6 and 8.
3.   There are infinitely many perfect numbers.

The next step forward came in 1603 when Cataldi could show that $2^{17}-1$ and $2^{19}-1$ are prime and therefore derived the 6th and 7th perfect numbers (see table below).

In 1732 Euler found the 8th perfect number (the first in 125 years). He also proved that every even perfect number must be from $2^{p-1}(2^p - 1)$. And that every even perfect number must end in either 6 or 8. Euler also tried to make some headway on the problem of whether odd perfect numbers existed.

As of 2003, 39 perfect numbers are known. It is not known if there are any odd perfect numbers. It has been shown that there are no odd perfect numbers in the interval from 1 to 10^{50}.

List of Perfect numbers based on Euler's formula: $2^{n-1}(2^n - 1)$			
	Perfect Number	Value of n	Formula
1	6	2	$2^1(2^2-1)$
2	28	3	$2^2(2^3-1)$
3	496	5	$2^4(2^5-1)$
4	8128	7	$2^6(2^7-1)$
5	33550336	13	$2^{12}(2^{13} - 1)$
6	8589869056	17	$2^{16}(2^{17} - 1)$
7	137438691328	19	$2^{18}(2^{19} - 1)$
8	2305843008139952128	31	$2^{30}(2^{31} - 1)$
9	265845599156983174465... ...4692615953842176	61	$2^{60}(2^{61} - 1)$

Squaring the Circle with Algebra

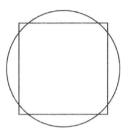

In esoteric thought, squaring the circle is the question of how matter (square) relates to spirit (circle). This is shown by finding a circle's circumference equal to a square's perimeter. With math and geometry, the problem is easy to solve.

Start with a circle with Radius = 1.

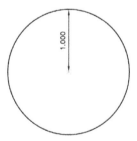

The circumference of a circle is the Diameter multiplied by Pi (π). The Diameter is twice the Radius.

$$D = 2R \qquad \text{Circumference} = 2\pi R$$

With the radius = 1, Circumference = 2π

Pi is an irrational number (a number that cannot be precisely defined) whose approximate value is 3.1416.

Now, find a square with the same perimeter.

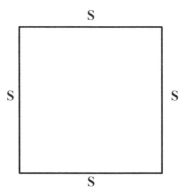

In a square, all sides are equal. Therefore the perimeter of a square is four times the length of a side.

Perimeter = 4S

Then we set the **Circumference** of the Circle equal to the **Perimeter** of the square.

$$\text{Circumference} = 2\pi R \qquad \text{Perimeter} = 4S$$

Therefore, $4S = 2\pi R$

With Radius = 1, the equation is $\qquad\qquad 4S = 2\pi$

To solve for S (side), we divide both sides of the equation by 4.

$$S = 2\pi/4$$

$S = \pi/2, \ \pi = 3.14159265...$

$S = 1.5708...$

And easy as pie, the problem is solved. However, Pi is an irrational number with no exact value, so how do you draw the squaring of the circle?

Squaring the Circle with Geometry

The Great Pyramid Giza

To solve the squaring of the circle geometrically, we need the third dimension.

Consider a circle with Radius = 1. Then the Height of the pyramid is 1. So the base's perimeter is 2π, and the length of each side is π / 2.

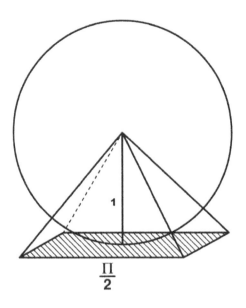

Note that the triangle that forms the pyramid's face is tilted approximately 32 degrees toward the pyramid's center.

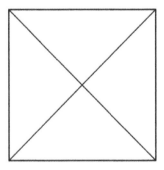

Top View of Pyramid

The only question remains: What does the triangle that makes up the pyramid look like?

The triangle's height is 1, and the base is π / 2.

We can see some interesting properties in the elevation view (side view) of the triangles that form the pyramid.

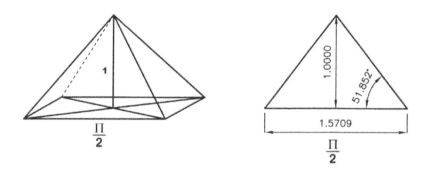

As seen from this perspective, the angle of the triangle is 51.85°, which is very close to the Great Pyramid in Gaza, Egypt – 51.84°.

From another perspective, we can see another interesting relationship.

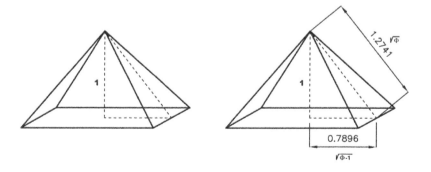

Phi (φ) is another irrational number with an approximate value of 1.618033988749895

Let's examine the interior triangle in more detail.

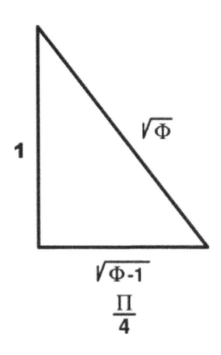

As an aside,

$\pi / 4 = 0.7854$

$\sqrt{(\phi - 1)} = 0.7862$

They are close but not the same.

Conclusion

Squaring the circle relates spirit (circle) to matter (square) from a philosophical perspective.

When performing this thought experiment using math and geometry, we require irrational numbers that never reach an exact solution. Squaring the circle is continually remembering and adjusting to the material world as a spiritual being.

Made in the USA
Coppell, TX
24 September 2024